Name ______________________________

Exercise 1A1

1. D	Owners	a.	Whether the firm can pay its bills on time.
2. b	Managers	b.	Detailed, up-to-date information to measure business performance (and plan for future operations).
3. a	Creditors	c.	To determine taxes to be paid and whether other regulations are met.
4. c	Government agencies	d.	The firm's current financial condition.

Exercise 1B1

Exercise 1A2

(1) Analyzing is looking to see what has happened and Thinking about how this affects the business.

(2) Recording is entering financial information into accounting system.

(3) Classifying is sorting and grouping like items together rather than merely keeping a simple, chain-like record of numerous events.

(4). Summerizing is bringing the various items of information together to explain a result

5. Reporting is telling the result. In accounting, it is common to use table of numbers to report result

6. Interpreting is deciding the importance of the various reports. This may include the percentage analyses and the use of ratios to help explian how pieces of information relate to one another.

Exercise 1B2

__________ Analyzing

__________ Recording

__________ Classifying

__________ Summarizing

__________ Reporting

__________ Interpreting

Exercise 2A1 or 2B1

Classification
A
A
L
A
OE
OE
A

✓

Exercise 2A2

Assets	=	Liabilities	+	Owner's Equity
34,000	=	$24,000	+	$10,000
$25,000	=	$18,000	+	7,000
$40,000	=	25,000	+	$15,000

Exercise 2B2

Assets	=	Liabilities	+	Owner's Equity
7,000	=	$20,000	+	$ 5,000
$30,000	=	$15,000	+	15,000
$20,000	=	10,000	+	$10,000

Exercise 2A3 or 2B3

	Assets	=	Liabilities	+	Owner's Equity
(a)	20,000				+20,000
Bal.	20,000				20,000
(b)	+3,500		$3,500		
Bal.	23,500		3,500		20,000
(c)	−1,200				
	1,200				
Bal.	$23,500		3,500		20,000
(d)	1,500		1,500		
Bal.	22,000		2,000		20,000

Exercise 2A4 or 2B4

	Assets	=	Liabilities	+	Owner's Equity						
					Capital	–	Drawing	+	Revenue	–	Expenses
Bal.											
(e)											
Bal.											
(f)											
Bal.											
(g)											
Bal.											
(h)											
Bal.											
(i)											
Bal.											
(j)											
Bal.											

Exercise 2A5 or 2B5

Account	Classification	Financial Statement	
Cash	A	Total	B
Rent Expense	x L E	expense	IS
Accounts Payable	L	expense	B
Service Fees	x A R	Revenue	IS
Supplies	A	Sub-Total	B
Wage Expense	A	W. expe	IS
John Smith, Drawing	OE		SOE
" ", Capital	OE		SOE, B
Prepaid Insurance	A		B
Accounts Receivable	A		B

Problem 2A1 or 2B1

	Assets	=	Liabilities	+	Owner's Equity
1.	47,00		2,420		11,880
2.			3,740		7,920
3.					6,200

Problem 2A2 or 2B2: See page 6

Problem 2A3 or 2B3

Income statement - for Albert - Hirsch

JOURNAL PAGE

	DATE		DESCRIPTION	POST. REF.	DEBIT	CREDIT	
1			Revenue			3300.00	1
2			expense			750.00	2
3							3
4			Net income			2550.00	4
5							5
6							6
7							7
8							8
9							9
10							10
11							11
12							12

Problem 2A2 or 2B2

	Assets			=	Liabilities	+	Owner's Equity						
	Cash	+	Office Equip.	=	Accounts Payable	+	Capital	−	Drawing	+	Revenue	−	Expenses
(a)	18,000						18,000						
Bal.	18,000												
(b)			4,600		+4,600								
Bal.	18,000		4,600		4,600		18,000						
(c)	−1,200		+1,200										
Bal.	16,800		5,800		4,600		18,000						
(d)	+3,300										+3,300		
Bal.	20,100		5,800		4,600		18,000				$3,300		
(e)	−2,300				−2,300								
Bal.	17,800		5,800		2,300		18,000				$3,300		
(f)	−750												+750
Bal.	17,050		5,800		2,300		18,000				$3,300		750
(g)	−100								+100				
Bal.	16,950				2,300		18,000		100		3,300		750

Total Assets cash 16,950
office equ 5,800
22,750

= Liabilities: Account payable $2,300
+ owner, equity 18,000
− Drawing 100
+ Revenue 3,300
− expens 750
22,750

Problem 2A4 or 2B4

Owners's equity for Albert-Hirsen
for month of April

Capital, April 1, 19		18000.00
Net income	2550.00	
Withdrawl for April	100.00	
		2450.00
Albert capital, April 30, 19		
		20450.00

9

Problem 2A5 or 2B5

Balance Sheet April 30, 19

Assets		Liabilities	
	16 950 00	Account payable	2300 00
Cash			
office eq	5800 00		
		Owners equity	
		Albert-Hirsen	
			20450 00
Total Assets	22 750 00	Total Lia + owners eq	20750 00

Mastery Problem

1.

	ASSETS Items Owned						= LIABILITIES + Amts. Owed	OWNER'S EQUITY Owner's Investment		Earnings		
	Cash +	Accts. Rec. +	Sup-plies +	Prepaid Ins. +	Tools +	Van =	Accts. Pay. +	L. Vozniak Capital −	L. Vozniak Drawing +	Revenue −	Expenses	Description
(a)												
Bal.												
(b)												
Bal.												
(c)												
Bal.												
(d)												
Bal.												
(e)												
Bal.												
(f)												
Bal.												
(g)												
Bal.												
(h)												
Bal.												
(i)												
Bal.												

Continued on next page

Mastery Problem (Continued)

Bal.
(j)
Bal.
(k)
Bal.
(l)
Bal.
(m)
Bal.
(n)
Bal.
(o)
Bal.
(p)
Bal.

2.

Mastery Problem (Continued)

3.

4.

Mastery Problem (Concluded)

5.

Name ______________________________

Exercise 3A1 or 3B1

a. Debit
b. Credit
c. debit
d. Credit
e. credit
f. credit
g. debit
h. debit
i. debit

Exercise 3A2 or 3B2

Arnold Basket corner

1. and 2.

Cash	
5,000	

Supplies	
800	

, Capital	
	5,000

Utilities Expense	
1,500	

Exercise 3A3 or 3B3

	Debit or Credit
1.	deb
2.	deb
3.	cre
4.	deb
5.	deb
6.	cre
7.	deb

Exercise 3A4 or 3B4

(a) Cash

Debit	Credit
4,000	

Sheryle Hase capital

Debit	Credit
	4,000

(b)

Debit	Credit
500	

Debit	Credit
	500

(c)

Debit	Credit
800	

Debit	Credit
	800

(d)

Debit	Credit
300	

Debit	Credit
	300

(e)

Debit	Credit
700	

Debit	Credit
	700

Exercise 3A5 or 3B5

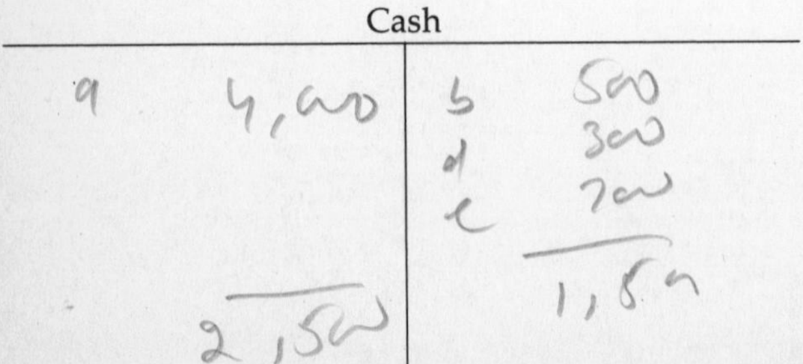

Cash

Debit	Credit
a 4,000	b 500
	d 300
	e 700
	1,500
2,500	

Exercise 3A6 or 3B6

Cash

DR	CR
a 30,000	b 300
e 3,000	c 5,000
J 6,000	f 4,000
	h. 15,000
	l 800
	K 3,000
	14,600

Accounts Receivable

DR	CR
e 3,000	J 6,000
g 3,000	

Office Supplies

b $300	

Computer Equipment

d, 8,000	

Office Furniture

c $5,000	

Accounts Payable

f 4,000	d, 8,000
	Bal 4,000

Professional Fees

	e 3,000
	g 9,000
	Bal 12,000

, Capital

	a 30,000

, Drawing

K 3,000	

Rent Expense

h 1,500	

Utility Expense

l 800	

Need to learn

Exercise 3A7 or 3B7

Charlie Detective service
Trial Balance
Jan 31, 19.

ACCOUNT	ACCT NO.	DEBIT BALANCE	CREDIT BALANCE
Cash		24,400 00	
Account recievable		3,000 00	
office supply		300 00	
Computer equipment		8000 00	
office Furniture		5000 00	
Account payable			400 00
Charles, Chadwick,s capital			30 000 00
, Drawing		3,000 00	
Professional fee			12 000 00
Rent expense		1500 00	
utility expenc		800 00	
		46 000 00	46000 00

Name May's Delivery Service

Exercise 3A8 or 3B8

Trial Balance
sep 30, 19

ACCOUNT	ACCT NO.	DEBIT BALANCE	CREDIT BALANCE
Cash		5,000	
Account Recievable		3,000	
Supplies		800	
Prepaid insurence		600	
Delivery equipment		8,000	
Account payable			2,000
Mary Jane's capitall			10,000
Mary " drawing		1,000	
Delivery Fees			9,400
Wages expense		2 100	
Rent expense		900	
		21 400	21 400

Exercise 3A9 or 3B9

Exercise 3A10 or 3B10

Exercise 3A11 or 3B11

Name ______________________________

Problem 3A1 or 3B1

1. and 2.

Problem 3A1 or 3B1 (Concluded)

3.

ACCOUNT	ACCT NO.	DEBIT BALANCE	CREDIT BALANCE

Problem 3A2 or 3B2

1.

(a) Total revenue for the month .... ________

(b) Total expense for the month .... ________

(c) Net income for the month .... ________

2.

(a) Owner's original investment in the business .... ________

Plus the net income for the month .... ________

Minus owner's drawing .... ________

Equals owner's equity at end of month .... ________

(b) End of month accounting equation:

Assets	=	Liabilities	+	Owner's Equity
________		________		________

Problem 3A3 or 3B3

1.

Problem 3A3 or 3B3 (Concluded)

2.

3.

Mastery Problem

1. and 2.: See pages 24–25.

3.

ACCOUNT	ACCT NO.	DEBIT BALANCE	CREDIT BALANCE

Mastery Problem (Continued)

1. and 2.

Assets		=	Liabilities		+
Dr. +	Cr. −		Dr. −	Cr. +	

Mastery Problem (Continued)

1. and 2.

Owner's Equity

Dr. −	Cr. +

Drawing	
Dr. +	Cr. −

Expenses	
Dr. +	Cr. −

Revenue	
Dr. −	Cr. +

Mastery Problem (Continued)

4.

Mastery Problem (Concluded)

5.

6.

Exercise 4A1

1. c Check stubs or check register
2. d Purchase invoice from suppliers (vendors)
3. a Sales tickets or invoices to customers
4. b Receipts of cash register tapes

Exercise 4B1

Exercise 4A2 or 4B2

	Debit	Credit
1.	cash 5000	Owner's equity
2.	Rent expense	~~revenue~~ cash
3.	office supplies	Account payable
4.	cash	Fees
5.	Account payable	cash
6.	cash	Account Recievable

Exercise 4A3 or 4B3

cash

Debit	Credit
1 5000	2. 500
4 400	5. 50
6 100	

office supply

3. 300	

Account payable

5. 50	3. 300

Acc Recieve cash revenue

	6. 100

Exercise 4A3 or 4B3 (Continued)

Fees	
	4. 400

Rent expense	
2. 500	

Owner's equity	
	1. 5,000

Exercise 4A4 or 4B4

JOURNAL PAGE 1

DATE		DESCRIPTION	POST. REF.	DEBIT	CREDIT
Jan 1993	1	Cash	111	10,000 00	
		Jean Jones capital	311		10,000
		owners investment			
	2	Rent expense	541	500 00	
		Office rent for	111		500 00
		Jan			
	3	Purchase office equipment	131	1,500 00	
		Acc payable	211		1,500 00
		purc office equip on account			
	5	Account recievable	111	750 00	
		service rendered	411		750 00
	8	Telephone expense	531	65 00	
		Telephone bill	111		65 00
	10	Miscellaneous exp	551	15 00	
		cash	111		15 00
		purchase magazine			
		subscription			

Name Zaheda

Exercise 4A4 or 4B4 (Continued)

JOURNAL

PAGE 2

DATE		DESCRIPTION	POST. REF.	DEBIT	CREDIT
1990 Jan	17	Office supplies	121	300 00	
		Account payable	211		300 00
		purchase office			
		supplies on account			
	15	Account payable	211	150 00	
		Cash	11		150 00
		Made p. payment			
		on office equip			
	18	Salary expense	521	500 —	
		cash	111		500 —
		paid emp			
	21	cash	111	3500 00	
		Fee			3500 00
		Revenue service			
	25	utilities	541	85 00	
		cash	111		85 00
		Paid Elec bill			
	27	Drawing	312	100 00	
		cash	111		100 00
		withdrawals			
	29	Salary expense	521	500 00	
		cash	111		500 —
		paid emp			

Exercise 4A4 or 4B4 (Concluded)

JOURNAL PAGE 3

	DATE		DESCRIPTION	POST. REF.	DEBIT	CREDIT	
1							1
2							2
3							3
4							4
5							5
6							6
7							7
8							8
9							9
10							10
11							11
12							12
13							13

Exercise 4A5 or 4B5

GENERAL LEDGER

ACCOUNT ACCOUNT NO.

DATE		ITEM	POST. REF.	DEBIT	CREDIT	BALANCE	
						DEBIT	CREDIT

Exercise 4A5 or 4B5 (Continued)

ACCOUNT ACCOUNT NO.

DATE		ITEM	POST. REF.	DEBIT	CREDIT	BALANCE	
						DEBIT	CREDIT

ACCOUNT ACCOUNT NO.

DATE		ITEM	POST. REF.	DEBIT	CREDIT	BALANCE	
						DEBIT	CREDIT

ACCOUNT ACCOUNT NO.

DATE		ITEM	POST. REF.	DEBIT	CREDIT	BALANCE	
						DEBIT	CREDIT

ACCOUNT ACCOUNT NO.

DATE		ITEM	POST. REF.	DEBIT	CREDIT	BALANCE	
						DEBIT	CREDIT

ACCOUNT ACCOUNT NO.

DATE		ITEM	POST. REF.	DEBIT	CREDIT	BALANCE	
						DEBIT	CREDIT

Exercise 4A5 or 4B5 (Continued)

ACCOUNT ACCOUNT NO.

DATE		ITEM	POST. REF.	DEBIT	CREDIT	BALANCE	
						DEBIT	CREDIT

ACCOUNT ACCOUNT NO.

DATE		ITEM	POST. REF.	DEBIT	CREDIT	BALANCE	
						DEBIT	CREDIT

ACCOUNT ACCOUNT NO.

DATE		ITEM	POST. REF.	DEBIT	CREDIT	BALANCE	
						DEBIT	CREDIT

ACCOUNT ACCOUNT NO.

DATE		ITEM	POST. REF.	DEBIT	CREDIT	BALANCE	
						DEBIT	CREDIT

Name ______________________________

Exercise 4A5 or 4B5 (Concluded)

ACCOUNT ACCOUNT NO.

DATE		ITEM	POST. REF.	DEBIT	CREDIT	BALANCE	
						DEBIT	CREDIT

ACCOUNT ACCOUNT NO.

DATE		ITEM	POST. REF.	DEBIT	CREDIT	BALANCE	
						DEBIT	CREDIT

ACCOUNT	ACCT NO.	DEBIT BALANCE	CREDIT BALANCE

Exercise 4A6 or 4B6 (Continued)

Exercise 4A6 or 4B6 (Concluded)

Exercise 4A7 or 4B7

Exercise 4A7 or 4B7 (Concluded)

Name ______________________________

Exercise 4A8

JOURNAL

PAGE

DATE		DESCRIPTION	POST. REF.	DEBIT	CREDIT
19-- May	17	*Office Equipment*		400 00	
		Cash			400 00
		Bought copy paper.			

JOURNAL

PAGE

DATE		DESCRIPTION	POST. REF.	DEBIT	CREDIT
19-- May	5	*Cash*	111	1 000 00	
		Service Fees	411		1 000 00
		Received cash for services			
		previously earned.			

Exercise 4B8

JOURNAL

PAGE

DATE		DESCRIPTION	POST. REF.	DEBIT	CREDIT
19-- Apr.	6	Office Supplies		530 00	
		Cash			530 00
		Purchased office equipment			
		on account.			

JOURNAL

PAGE

DATE		DESCRIPTION	POST. REF.	DEBIT	CREDIT
19-- Apr.	2	Cash	111	300 00	
		Service Fees	411		300 00
		Fees earned.			

DATE		DESCRIPTION	POST. REF.	DEBIT	CREDIT
Apr.	25				

Problem 4A1 or 4B1

1.

JOURNAL PAGE 7

	DATE		DESCRIPTION	POST. REF.	DEBIT	CREDIT	
1							1
2							2
3							3
4							4
5							5
6							6
7							7
8							8
9							9
10							10
11							11
12							12
13							13
14							14
15							15
16							16
17							17
18							18
19							19
20							20
21							21
22							22
23							23
24							24
25							25
26							26
27							27
28							28
29							29
30							30
31							31
32							32

Problem 4A1 or 4B1 (Continued)

JOURNAL

PAGE 8

DATE		DESCRIPTION	POST. REF.	DEBIT	CREDIT

Name ______________________________

Problem 4A1 or 4B1 (Continued)

JOURNAL

PAGE 9

	DATE		DESCRIPTION	POST. REF.	DEBIT	CREDIT	
1							1
2							2
3							3
4							4
5							5
6							6
7							7
8							8
9							9
10							10
11							11
12							12
13							13
14							14
15							15
16							16
17							17
18							18
19							19
20							20
21							21
22							22
23							23
24							24
25							25
26							26
27							27
28							28
29							29
30							30
31							31
32							32

Problem 4A1 or 4B1 (Continued)

2.

GENERAL LEDGER

ACCOUNT ACCOUNT NO.

DATE		ITEM	POST. REF.	DEBIT	CREDIT	BALANCE	
						DEBIT	CREDIT

Problem 4A1 or 4B1 (Continued)

ACCOUNT ACCOUNT NO.

DATE		ITEM	POST. REF.	DEBIT	CREDIT	BALANCE	
						DEBIT	CREDIT

ACCOUNT ACCOUNT NO.

DATE		ITEM	POST. REF.	DEBIT	CREDIT	BALANCE	
						DEBIT	CREDIT

ACCOUNT ACCOUNT NO.

DATE		ITEM	POST. REF.	DEBIT	CREDIT	BALANCE	
						DEBIT	CREDIT

Problem 4A1 or 4B1 (Continued)

ACCOUNT ACCOUNT NO.

DATE	ITEM	POST. REF.	DEBIT	CREDIT	BALANCE	
					DEBIT	CREDIT

ACCOUNT ACCOUNT NO.

DATE	ITEM	POST. REF.	DEBIT	CREDIT	BALANCE	
					DEBIT	CREDIT

ACCOUNT ACCOUNT NO.

DATE	ITEM	POST. REF.	DEBIT	CREDIT	BALANCE	
					DEBIT	CREDIT

ACCOUNT ACCOUNT NO.

DATE	ITEM	POST. REF.	DEBIT	CREDIT	BALANCE	
					DEBIT	CREDIT

Name ______________________________

Problem 4A1 or 4B1 (Continued)

ACCOUNT ACCOUNT NO.

DATE		ITEM	POST. REF.	DEBIT	CREDIT	BALANCE DEBIT	BALANCE CREDIT

ACCOUNT ACCOUNT NO.

DATE		ITEM	POST. REF.	DEBIT	CREDIT	BALANCE DEBIT	BALANCE CREDIT

ACCOUNT ACCOUNT NO.

DATE		ITEM	POST. REF.	DEBIT	CREDIT	BALANCE DEBIT	BALANCE CREDIT

ACCOUNT ACCOUNT NO.

DATE		ITEM	POST. REF.	DEBIT	CREDIT	BALANCE DEBIT	BALANCE CREDIT

Problem 4A1 or 4B1 (Continued)

ACCOUNT ACCOUNT NO.

DATE		ITEM	POST. REF.	DEBIT	CREDIT	BALANCE DEBIT	BALANCE CREDIT

ACCOUNT ACCOUNT NO.

DATE		ITEM	POST. REF.	DEBIT	CREDIT	BALANCE DEBIT	BALANCE CREDIT

ACCOUNT ACCOUNT NO.

DATE		ITEM	POST. REF.	DEBIT	CREDIT	BALANCE DEBIT	BALANCE CREDIT

ACCOUNT ACCOUNT NO.

DATE		ITEM	POST. REF.	DEBIT	CREDIT	BALANCE DEBIT	BALANCE CREDIT

ACCOUNT ACCOUNT NO.

DATE		ITEM	POST. REF.	DEBIT	CREDIT	BALANCE DEBIT	BALANCE CREDIT

Name ______________________

Problem 4A1 or 4B1 (Continued)

3.

ACCOUNT	ACCT NO.	DEBIT BALANCE	CREDIT BALANCE

Problem 4A1 or 4B1 (Continued)

4.

Name ______________________________

Problem 4A1 or 4B1 (Continued)

5.

Problem 4A2 or 4B2

1.

JOURNAL PAGE 1

DATE	DESCRIPTION	POST. REF.	DEBIT	CREDIT

Name ____________________

Problem 4A2 or 4B2 (Continued)

JOURNAL PAGE 2

	DATE		DESCRIPTION	POST. REF.	DEBIT	CREDIT	
1							1
2							2
3							3
4							4
5							5
6							6
7							7
8							8
9							9
10							10
11							11
12							12
13							13
14							14
15							15
16							16
17							17
18							18
19							19
20							20
21							21
22							22
23							23
24							24
25							25
26							26
27							27
28							28
29							29
30							30
31							31
32							32
33							33
34							34

Problem 4A2 or 4B2 (Continued)

JOURNAL

PAGE 3

DATE		DESCRIPTION	POST. REF.	DEBIT	CREDIT

Name ______________________________

Problem 4A2 or 4B2 (Continued)

2.

GENERAL LEDGER

ACCOUNT ACCOUNT NO.

DATE		ITEM	POST. REF.	DEBIT	CREDIT	BALANCE	
						DEBIT	CREDIT

ACCOUNT ACCOUNT NO.

DATE		ITEM	POST. REF.	DEBIT	CREDIT	BALANCE	
						DEBIT	CREDIT

Problem 4A2 or 4B2 (Continued)

ACCOUNT ACCOUNT NO.

DATE		ITEM	POST. REF.	DEBIT	CREDIT	BALANCE DEBIT	BALANCE CREDIT

ACCOUNT ACCOUNT NO.

DATE		ITEM	POST. REF.	DEBIT	CREDIT	BALANCE DEBIT	BALANCE CREDIT

ACCOUNT ACCOUNT NO.

DATE		ITEM	POST. REF.	DEBIT	CREDIT	BALANCE DEBIT	BALANCE CREDIT

ACCOUNT ACCOUNT NO.

DATE		ITEM	POST. REF.	DEBIT	CREDIT	BALANCE DEBIT	BALANCE CREDIT

Problem 4A2 or 4B2 (Continued)

ACCOUNT ACCOUNT NO.

DATE		ITEM	POST. REF.	DEBIT	CREDIT	BALANCE	
						DEBIT	CREDIT

ACCOUNT ACCOUNT NO.

DATE		ITEM	POST. REF.	DEBIT	CREDIT	BALANCE	
						DEBIT	CREDIT

ACCOUNT ACCOUNT NO.

DATE		ITEM	POST. REF.	DEBIT	CREDIT	BALANCE	
						DEBIT	CREDIT

ACCOUNT ACCOUNT NO.

DATE		ITEM	POST. REF.	DEBIT	CREDIT	BALANCE	
						DEBIT	CREDIT

Problem 4A2 or 4B2 (Continued)

ACCOUNT ACCOUNT NO.

DATE		ITEM	POST. REF.	DEBIT	CREDIT	BALANCE DEBIT	BALANCE CREDIT

ACCOUNT ACCOUNT NO.

DATE		ITEM	POST. REF.	DEBIT	CREDIT	BALANCE DEBIT	BALANCE CREDIT

ACCOUNT ACCOUNT NO.

DATE		ITEM	POST. REF.	DEBIT	CREDIT	BALANCE DEBIT	BALANCE CREDIT

ACCOUNT ACCOUNT NO.

DATE		ITEM	POST. REF.	DEBIT	CREDIT	BALANCE DEBIT	BALANCE CREDIT

ACCOUNT ACCOUNT NO.

DATE		ITEM	POST. REF.	DEBIT	CREDIT	BALANCE DEBIT	BALANCE CREDIT

Problem 4A2 or 4B2 (Continued)

3.

ACCOUNT	ACCT NO.	DEBIT BALANCE	CREDIT BALANCE

Problem 4A2 or 4B2 (Continued)

4.

Problem 4A2 or 4B2 (Concluded)

Problem 4A3 or 4B3

Problem 4A3 or 4B3 (Concluded)

Mastery Problem

1.

JOURNAL

PAGE 1

DATE	DESCRIPTION	POST. REF.	DEBIT	CREDIT

Mastery Problem (Continued)

JOURNAL

PAGE 2

DATE		DESCRIPTION	POST. REF.	DEBIT	CREDIT

Mastery Problem (Continued)

JOURNAL PAGE 3

DATE		DESCRIPTION	POST. REF.	DEBIT	CREDIT

Name ____________________

Mastery Problem (Continued)

2.

GENERAL LEDGER

ACCOUNT ACCOUNT NO.

DATE		ITEM	POST. REF.	DEBIT	CREDIT	BALANCE DEBIT	BALANCE CREDIT

ACCOUNT ACCOUNT NO.

DATE		ITEM	POST. REF.	DEBIT	CREDIT	BALANCE DEBIT	BALANCE CREDIT

Mastery Problem (Continued)

ACCOUNT ACCOUNT NO.

DATE		ITEM	POST. REF.	DEBIT	CREDIT	BALANCE DEBIT	BALANCE CREDIT

ACCOUNT ACCOUNT NO.

DATE		ITEM	POST. REF.	DEBIT	CREDIT	BALANCE DEBIT	BALANCE CREDIT

ACCOUNT ACCOUNT NO.

DATE		ITEM	POST. REF.	DEBIT	CREDIT	BALANCE DEBIT	BALANCE CREDIT

ACCOUNT ACCOUNT NO.

DATE		ITEM	POST. REF.	DEBIT	CREDIT	BALANCE DEBIT	BALANCE CREDIT

Mastery Problem (Continued)

ACCOUNT ACCOUNT NO.

DATE		ITEM	POST. REF.	DEBIT	CREDIT	BALANCE	
						DEBIT	CREDIT

ACCOUNT ACCOUNT NO.

DATE		ITEM	POST. REF.	DEBIT	CREDIT	BALANCE	
						DEBIT	CREDIT

ACCOUNT ACCOUNT NO.

DATE		ITEM	POST. REF.	DEBIT	CREDIT	BALANCE	
						DEBIT	CREDIT

ACCOUNT ACCOUNT NO.

DATE		ITEM	POST. REF.	DEBIT	CREDIT	BALANCE	
						DEBIT	CREDIT

Mastery Problem (Concluded)

ACCOUNT ACCOUNT NO.

DATE		ITEM	POST. REF.	DEBIT	CREDIT	BALANCE	
						DEBIT	CREDIT

ACCOUNT ACCOUNT NO.

DATE		ITEM	POST. REF.	DEBIT	CREDIT	BALANCE	
						DEBIT	CREDIT

3.

ACCOUNT	ACCT NO.	DEBIT BALANCE	CREDIT BALANCE

Name Zahedi

Exercise 5A1 or 5B1

(Balance Sheet) Supplies		(Income Statement) Supplies Expense	
TB 635	Adj 635	Adj 635	
90			
?			

JOURNAL PAGE

	DATE		DESCRIPTION	POST. REF.	DEBIT	CREDIT	
1			Adjusting entries				1
2	19 Dec	31	supplies expense		635 —		2
3			supplies			635 —	3
4							4
5							5
6							6

Exercise 5A2 or 5B2

(Balance Sheet) Prepaid Insurance		(Income Statement) Insurance Expense	
TB 980	Adj 130	Adj 130	
Bal 130			
850			

850
130
720

JOURNAL PAGE

	DATE		DESCRIPTION	POST. REF.	DEBIT	CREDIT	
1			Adjusting entries				1
2	Dec	31	Insurance expense		130 —		2
3			prepaid insurance			130 —	3
4							4
5							5
6							6

Exercise 5A3 or 5B3

(Income Statement)
Wage Expense

TB 1,800	
Adj 180	
BAL 1,620	

(Balance Sheet)
Wages Payable

	Adj 180

JOURNAL

PAGE

	DATE		DESCRIPTION	POST. REF.	DEBIT	CREDIT	
1	Dec	31	Adjusting entry				1
2			Wages exp		180 00		2
3			Wages payable			180 00	3
4							4

Exercise 5A4 or 5B4

1,440 × 1/48? = ______

(Income Statement)
Depr. Expense—Delivery Equip.

Adj —	

(Balance Sheet)
Accum. Depr.—Delivery Equip.

	Adj —

JOURNAL

PAGE

	DATE		DESCRIPTION	POST. REF.	DEBIT	CREDIT	
1			Adjusting entries				1
2	Dec	31	Depr exp - Deli equip		—		2
3			Accum depr - Delivery equ.			—	3
4							4

Exercise 5A5 or 5B5

Exercise 5A6 or 5B6

1.

(Balance Sheet) Supplies		(Income Statement) Supplies Expense	

2.

(Balance Sheet) Supplies		(Income Statement) Supplies Expense	

Exercise 5A7 or 5B7

1.

(Balance Sheet) Prepaid Insurance		(Income Statement) Insurance Expense	

2.

(Balance Sheet) Prepaid Insurance		(Income Statement) Insurance Expense	

Exercise 5A8 or 5B8

	ACCOUNT TITLE	ACCT. NO.	TRIAL BALANCE		ADJUSTMENTS		ADJ. TRIAL BALANCE		
			DEBIT	CREDIT	DEBIT	CREDIT	DEBIT	CREDIT	
1	*Cash*								1
2	*Supplies*								2
3	*Prepaid Insurance*								3
4	*Equipment*								4
5	*Accum. Dep.—Equip.*								5
6	*, Capital*								6
7	*Sales Revenue*								7
8	*Wage Expense*								8
9	*Advertising Expense*								9
10									10
11	*Supplies Expense*								11
12	*Insurance Expense*								12
13	*Dep. Exp.—Equip.*								13
14	*Wages Payable*								14
15									15
16									16
17									17
18									18
19									19

Name ____________________

Exercise 5A9 or 5B9

JOURNAL PAGE

	DATE		DESCRIPTION	POST. REF.	DEBIT	CREDIT	
1							1
2							2
3							3
4							4
5							5
6							6
7							7
8							8
9							9
10							10
11							11
12							12
13							13
14							14

Exercise 5A10 or 5B10

JOURNAL PAGE

	DATE		DESCRIPTION	POST. REF.	DEBIT	CREDIT	
1							1
2							2
3							3
4							4
5							5
6							6
7							7
8							8
9							9
10							10
11							11
12							12
13							13
14							14

Exercise 5A10 or 5B10 (Concluded)

GENERAL LEDGER

ACCOUNT ACCOUNT NO.

DATE		ITEM	POST. REF.	DEBIT	CREDIT	BALANCE	
						DEBIT	CREDIT

ACCOUNT ACCOUNT NO.

DATE		ITEM	POST. REF.	DEBIT	CREDIT	BALANCE	
						DEBIT	CREDIT

ACCOUNT ACCOUNT NO.

DATE		ITEM	POST. REF.	DEBIT	CREDIT	BALANCE	
						DEBIT	CREDIT

ACCOUNT ACCOUNT NO.

DATE		ITEM	POST. REF.	DEBIT	CREDIT	BALANCE	
						DEBIT	CREDIT

Name ______________________________

Exercise 5A11 or 5B11

Account Title	Income Statement Dr.	Income Statement Cr.	Balance Sheet Dr.	Balance Sheet Cr.
Cash				
Accounts Receivable				
Supplies				
Prepaid Insurance				
Delivery Equip. (5A11) or Automobile (5B11)				
Accounts Payable				
Owner's Capital				
Owner's Drawing				
Delivery Fees (5A11) or Service Income (5B11)				
Rent Expense (5A11) or Utilities Expense (5B11)				
Wage Expense				
Supplies Expense				
Insurance Expense				
Wages Payable				
Depr. Exp.—Del. Equip. (5A11) or Depr. Exp.—Auto (5B11)				
Accum. Depr.—Del. Equip. (5A11) or Accum. Depr.—Auto (5B11)				

Exercise 5A12 or 5B12

Account Title	Income Statement Dr.	Income Statement Cr.	Balance Sheet Dr.	Balance Sheet Cr.
Net Income				
Net Loss				

Problem 5A1 or 5B1

	ACCOUNT TITLE	ACCT. NO.	TRIAL BALANCE		ADJUSTMENTS		
			DEBIT	CREDIT	DEBIT	CREDIT	
1							1
2							2
3							3
4							4
5							5
6							6
7							7
8							8
9							9
10							10
11							11
12							12
13							13
14							14
15							15
16							16
17							17
18							18
19							19
20							20
21							21
22							22
23							23
24							24
25							25
26							26
27							27
28							28
29							29
30							30
31							31
32							32

Name ____

Problem 5A1 or 5B1 (Concluded)

	ADJUSTED TRIAL BALANCE		INCOME STATEMENT		BALANCE SHEET		
	DEBIT	CREDIT	DEBIT	CREDIT	DEBIT	CREDIT	
1							1
2							2
3							3
4							4
5							5
6							6
7							7
8							8
9							9
10							10
11							11
12							12
13							13
14							14
15							15
16							16
17							17
18							18
19							19
20							20
21							21
22							22
23							23
24							24
25							25
26							26
27							27
28							28
29							29
30							30
31							31
32							32

Problem 5A2 or 5B2

	ACCOUNT TITLE	ACCT. NO.	TRIAL BALANCE		ADJUSTMENTS		
			DEBIT	CREDIT	DEBIT	CREDIT	
1							1
2							2
3							3
4							4
5							5
6							6
7							7
8							8
9							9
10							10
11							11
12							12
13							13
14							14
15							15
16							16
17							17
18							18
19							19
20							20
21							21
22							22
23							23
24							24
25							25
26							26
27							27
28							28
29							29
30							30
31							31
32							32

Name ____________________

Problem 5A2 or 5B2 (Concluded)

ADJUSTED TRIAL BALANCE		INCOME STATEMENT		BALANCE SHEET	
DEBIT	CREDIT	DEBIT	CREDIT	DEBIT	CREDIT

Problem 5A3 or 5B3: **See pages 84–86**

Problem 5A4 or 5B4

	ACCOUNT TITLE	ACCT. NO.	TRIAL BALANCE		ADJUSTMENTS		
			DEBIT	CREDIT	DEBIT	CREDIT	
1	*Cash*						1
2	*Accounts Receivable*						2
3	*Supplies*						3
4	*Prepaid Insurance*						4
5	*Office Equipment*						5
6	*Accounts Payable*						6
7	*, Capital*						7
8	*, Drawing*						8
9	*Professional Fees*						9
10	*Rent Expense*						10
11	*Wage Expense*						11
12	*Telephone Expense*						12
13	*Utilities Expense*						13
14	*Advertising Expense*						14
15	*Miscellaneous Expense*						15
16							16
17	*Supplies Expense*						17
18	*Insurance Expense*						18
19	*Dep. Exp.—Office Equip.*						19
20	*Accum. Dep.—Office Equip.*						20
21	*Wages Payable*						21
22							22
23	***Net Income***						23
24							24
25							25
26							26
27							27
28							28
29							29

Problem 5A4 or 5B4 (Concluded)

	ADJUSTED TRIAL BALANCE		INCOME STATEMENT		BALANCE SHEET		
	DEBIT	CREDIT	DEBIT	CREDIT	DEBIT	CREDIT	
1							1
2							2
3							3
4							4
5							5
6							6
7							7
8							8
9							9
10							10
11							11
12							12
13							13
14							14
15							15
16							16
17							17
18							18
19							19
20							20
21							21
22							22
23							23
24							24
25							25
26							26
27							27
28							28
29							29

Problem 5A3 or 5B3

1.

JOURNAL

PAGE

	DATE		DESCRIPTION	POST. REF.	DEBIT	CREDIT	
1							1
2							2
3							3
4							4
5							5
6							6
7							7
8							8
9							9
10							10
11							11
12							12
13							13
14							14
15							15
16							16
17							17
18							18
19							19
20							20
21							21
22							22
23							23
24							24
25							25
26							26
27							27
28							28
29							29
30							30
31							31
32							32

Name ____________________

Problem 5A3 or 5B3 (Continued)

2.

GENERAL LEDGER

ACCOUNT ____________________ ACCOUNT NO. ______

DATE	ITEM	POST. REF.	DEBIT	CREDIT	BALANCE DEBIT	BALANCE CREDIT

ACCOUNT ____________________ ACCOUNT NO. ______

DATE	ITEM	POST. REF.	DEBIT	CREDIT	BALANCE DEBIT	BALANCE CREDIT

ACCOUNT ____________________ ACCOUNT NO. ______

DATE	ITEM	POST. REF.	DEBIT	CREDIT	BALANCE DEBIT	BALANCE CREDIT

ACCOUNT ____________________ ACCOUNT NO. ______

DATE	ITEM	POST. REF.	DEBIT	CREDIT	BALANCE DEBIT	BALANCE CREDIT

Problem 5A3 or 5B3 (Concluded)

ACCOUNT ACCOUNT NO.

DATE	ITEM	POST. REF.	DEBIT	CREDIT	BALANCE	
					DEBIT	CREDIT

ACCOUNT ACCOUNT NO.

DATE	ITEM	POST. REF.	DEBIT	CREDIT	BALANCE	
					DEBIT	CREDIT

ACCOUNT ACCOUNT NO.

DATE	ITEM	POST. REF.	DEBIT	CREDIT	BALANCE	
					DEBIT	CREDIT

ACCOUNT ACCOUNT NO.

DATE	ITEM	POST. REF.	DEBIT	CREDIT	BALANCE	
					DEBIT	CREDIT

Mastery Problem

1. and 2.: See pages 88–89

3.

JOURNAL PAGE

	DATE		DESCRIPTION	POST. REF.	DEBIT	CREDIT	
1							1
2							2
3							3
4							4
5							5
6							6
7							7
8							8
9							9
10							10
11							11
12							12
13							13
14							14
15							15
16							16
17							17
18							18
19							19
20							20
21							21
22							22
23							23
24							24
25							25
26							26
27							27
28							28
29							29
30							30
31							31

Mastery Problem (Continued)

1. and 2.

Kristi Williams

Work

For the Month Ended

ACCOUNT TITLE	ACCT. NO.	TRIAL BALANCE DEBIT	TRIAL BALANCE CREDIT	ADJUSTMENTS DEBIT	ADJUSTMENTS CREDIT
Cash		8,730.00			
Office Supplies		700.00			
Prepaid Insurance		600.00			
Office Equipment		18,000.00			
Computer Equipment		6,000.00			
Notes Payable			8,000.00		
Accounts Payable			500.00		
Kristi Williams, Capital			11,400.00		
Kristi Williams, Drawing		3,000.00			
Client Fees			35,800.00		
Rent Expense		6,000.00			
Salary Expense		9,500.00			
Utility Expense		2,170.00			
Charitable Contr. Exp.		1,000.00			
		55,700.00	55,700.00		
Office Supplies Expense					
Depr. Exp.—Office Equip.					
Accum. Depr.—Computer Equip.					
Depr. Exp.—Computer Equip.					
Accum. Depr.—Computer Equip.					
Insurance Expense					
Net Income					

Mastery Problem (Concluded)

Family Counseling Services

Sheet

December 31, 19--

ADJUSTED TRIAL BALANCE		INCOME STATEMENT		BALANCE SHEET	
DEBIT	CREDIT	DEBIT	CREDIT	DEBIT	CREDIT

Name Zaheder

Exercise 6A1 or 6B1

Bill case

Month Jan

Exercise 6A2 or 6B2

Exercise 6A3 or 6B3

Name ______________________________

Exercise 6A4 or 6B4

JOURNAL

PAGE

	DATE		DESCRIPTION	POST. REF.	DEBIT	CREDIT	
1							1
2							2
3							3
4							4
5							5
6							6
7							7
8							8
9							9
10							10
11							11
12							12
13							13
14							14
15							15
16							16
17							17
18							18
19							19
20							20
21							21
22							22

Exercise 6A4 or 6B4 (Concluded)

Name ______________________________

Exercise 6A5 or 6B5

JOURNAL

PAGE

DATE		DESCRIPTION	POST. REF.	DEBIT	CREDIT

Exercise 6A5 or 6B5 (Concluded)

Name Zahedi

Problem 6A1 or 6B1

1.

Bill case
Income statement
For Month Ended Jan 31, -- 1993

Revenue		
Delivery Fee		$3 793 00
expense		
wages expense	800 00	
Rent expense	500 00	
supplies expense	120 00	
Depr-exp - del. equip	100 00	
Advertising exp	80 00	
Telephone exp	58 00	
Electricity exp	49 00	
Gas & oil exp	38 00	
Insurance exp	30 00	
Miscellaneous exp	33 00	
Total expense		1 803 00
Net Income		1 990 00

2.

Bill Case
Income statement
For the month of Jan 31 1993

Bill case capital Jan 31		$4 000 00
Net Income for Jan	1 990 00	
Less withdrawals	800 00	
		1 190 00
Bill case capital Jan 31,		$5 190 00

Problem 6A1 or 6B1 (Concluded)

3.

Bill Case Repair
Balance Sheet
Jan 31, 19--

Current Assets		
Cash	$1212 00	
Account Receivable	896 00	
Supplies	482 00	
Prepaid insurance	900 00	
Total current Assets		3490 00
Property, plant & equipment		
Delivery equipment	$3000 00	
Less: Accumulated depreciation	100 00	2900 00
Total Assets		6390 00
Liabilities		
Current Liabilities		
Account payable	1000 00	
Wages payable	200 00	
Total current Liabilities		1200 00
Owner's Equity		
Monty's Repair, capital		5190 00
Total Liabilities and owner's equity		$6390 00

Name Zobeda

Problem 6A2 or 6B2

Jessi Richards
Statement of owners equity
For month Jan 31

Jessie Richard capital Jan 1, 19		4 800 00
Add: Additional investment		1 200 00
Total investment		6 000 00
Net income for Jan	1 820 00	
Less withdrawal	1 000 00	
increase in capital		820 00
Jessie Richards capital Jan 31, 19		6 820 00

Problem 6A3 or 6B3

1.

JOURNAL PAGE 10

DATE		DESCRIPTION	POST. REF.	DEBIT	CREDIT
Jan		Adjusting entries			
	31	supplies exp	543	200 00	
		Supplies	151		200 00
	31	Insurance exp	548	100 00	
		prepaid	155		100 00
	31	salary exp	542	150 00	
		salary payable	219		150 00
	31	Depr. exp. Del equipment	547	30 00	
		Accum. depr - Del. eq	185.1		30 00

Problem 6A3 or 6B3 (Continued)

2.

JOURNAL PAGE 11

DATE		DESCRIPTION	POST. REF.	DEBIT	CREDIT
Jan	31	Closing entries			
		Repair Fees	411	4230 00	
		Income Summary	313		4230 00
	31	Income Summary	313	1760 00	
		Rent exp	541		420
		Salary "	542		800 00
		Telep "	545		49 00
		Gas & Oil "	550		33 00
		Advertising "	551		100 00
		Miscellaneous "	572		25 00
		supplies "	543		200 —
		Insurance exp	548		100 —
		depr. exp- Del. 294	547		300 —
	31	Income summary	313	2470 00	
		Monti Eli, capital	311		2470 00
	31	Monti E, capital	311	1000	
		" Drawing	312		1000 00

3.

GENERAL LEDGER

ACCOUNT Cash ACCOUNT NO. 111

DATE		ITEM	POST. REF.	DEBIT	CREDIT	BALANCE DEBIT	BALANCE CREDIT
Jan	31		✓			915 00	

Name ______________________________

Problem 6A3 or 6B3 (Continued)

ACCOUNT Account Recievable ACCOUNT NO. 131

DATE		ITEM	POST. REF.	DEBIT	CREDIT	BALANCE	
						DEBIT	CREDIT
Jan	31		✓			1 200 00	

ACCOUNT Supplies ACCOUNT NO. 151

DATE		ITEM	POST. REF.	DEBIT	CREDIT	BALANCE	
						DEBIT	CREDIT
Jan	31		✓			800 00	
		Adjusting	J10		200 00	600 00	

ACCOUNT Prepaid insurance ACCOUNT NO. 155

DATE		ITEM	POST. REF.	DEBIT	CREDIT	BALANCE	
						DEBIT	CREDIT
Jan	31		✓			900	
			J10		100	800	

ACCOUNT Delivery equipment ACCOUNT NO. 185

DATE		ITEM	POST. REF.	DEBIT	CREDIT	BALANCE	
						DEBIT	CREDIT
Jan	31		✓			3000 —	

ACCOUNT Account payable ACCOUNT NO. 211

DATE		ITEM	POST. REF.	DEBIT	CREDIT	BALANCE	
						DEBIT	CREDIT
			✓			3 000 —	1 110 —

Problem 6A3 or 6B3 (Continued)

ACCOUNT Delivery Equip ACCOUNT NO. 185

DATE		ITEM	POST. REF.	DEBIT	CREDIT	BALANCE DEBIT	BALANCE CREDIT
Jan	31		J10		300 —		300 —

ACCOUNT Monti. Sli Capital ACCOUNT NO. 311

DATE		ITEM	POST. REF.	DEBIT	CREDIT	BALANCE DEBIT	BALANCE CREDIT
Jan	31		J11				6 000 00
	31	closing	J11				8 470 —
	31	closing					7 470 00

ACCOUNT Monti. Sli Drawing ACCOUNT NO. 312

DATE		ITEM	POST. REF.	DEBIT	CREDIT	BALANCE DEBIT	BALANCE CREDIT
Jan	31					1 000 00	
		closing	J11		1 000 00	—	—

ACCOUNT Salary payable ACCOUNT NO. 214

DATE		ITEM	POST. REF.	DEBIT	CREDIT	BALANCE DEBIT	BALANCE CREDIT
Jan	31	Ad	J10		150 —		150 —

ACCOUNT ACCOUNT NO.

DATE		ITEM	POST. REF.	DEBIT	CREDIT	BALANCE DEBIT	BALANCE CREDIT

Name ______________________________

Problem 6A3 or 6B3 (Continued)

ACCOUNT Repair Fees ACCOUNT NO. 411

DATE		ITEM	POST. REF.	DEBIT	CREDIT	BALANCE DEBIT	BALANCE CREDIT
Jan	31	✓					4 230 00
		Closing	J11	4 230 00			

ACCOUNT Rent expense ACCOUNT NO. 541

DATE		ITEM	POST. REF.	DEBIT	CREDIT	BALANCE DEBIT	BALANCE CREDIT
Jan	31					420 00	
	31	Closing	J11		420	—	—

ACCOUNT Salary expense ACCOUNT NO. 542

DATE		ITEM	POST. REF.	DEBIT	CREDIT	BALANCE DEBIT	BALANCE CREDIT
Jan	31					650 00	
		Adj	J10	150 00		800	
		Clos	J11		800 00	—	—

ACCOUNT Supplies ACCOUNT NO. 543

DATE		ITEM	POST. REF.	DEBIT	CREDIT	BALANCE DEBIT	BALANCE CREDIT
Jan	31	Ad	J10	200 00		200	
		Clo	J11		200	—	—

ACCOUNT ACCOUNT NO. 545

DATE		ITEM	POST. REF.	DEBIT	CREDIT	BALANCE DEBIT	BALANCE CREDIT
Jan	31		✓			49 00	
	31	Closing	J11		49	—	—

Problem 6A3 or 6B3 (Continued)

ACCOUNT Dep exp ACCOUNT NO. 547

DATE		ITEM	POST. REF.	DEBIT	CREDIT	BALANCE	
						DEBIT	CREDIT
Jan	31	Ad	J10	30		30 —	
		Clo	J11		30 —	—	—

ACCOUNT Insurance exp ACCOUNT NO. 548

DATE		ITEM	POST. REF.	DEBIT	CREDIT	BALANCE	
						DEBIT	CREDIT
Jan	31	Ad	J10	100 —		100	
		Clo	J10		100 —	—	—

ACCOUNT Gas oil ACCOUNT NO. 550

DATE		ITEM	POST. REF.	DEBIT	CREDIT	BALANCE	
						DEBIT	CREDIT
Jan	31	Ad	J10			830	
		Closing	J11		830	—	—

ACCOUNT Advertising exp ACCOUNT NO.

DATE		ITEM	POST. REF.	DEBIT	CREDIT	BALANCE	
						DEBIT	CREDIT
Jan	31		✓			100	
	31	closing	J11		100	—	—

ACCOUNT Misalleneous ACCOUNT NO.

DATE		ITEM	POST. REF.	DEBIT	CREDIT	BALANCE	
						DEBIT	CREDIT
Jan	31		✓			260	
	31	Clos	J11		260 —	—	—

Name

Problem 6A3 or 6B3 (Concluded)

ACCOUNT ACCOUNT NO.

DATE		ITEM	POST. REF.	DEBIT	CREDIT	BALANCE DEBIT	BALANCE CREDIT

4.

Mont's Repair
post - closing Trial Bal

ACCOUNT	ACCT NO.	DEBIT BALANCE	CREDIT BALANCE
Cash	111	315 —	
Account Recievels	131	1 200 —	
Supplies	151	600 —	
Pre paid Ins	155	800 —	
Del. Equipment	185	3 000 —	
Accumulated Dep - Del. Eq	185.1		30 —
Accounts payable	211		1 100 —
Salary payable	219		150 —
Mont's; capital	311		7 470 —
		8 750 —	8 750 —

Mastery Problem

Mastery Problem (Continued)

Mastery Problem (Concluded)

JOURNAL

PAGE

DATE		DESCRIPTION	POST. REF.	DEBIT	CREDIT

Name ______________________________

Comprehensive Problem 1

1.

JOURNAL PAGE *1*

DATE	DESCRIPTION	POST. REF.	DEBIT	CREDIT

Comprehensive Problem 1 (Continued)

JOURNAL PAGE 2

	DATE	DESCRIPTION	POST. REF.	DEBIT	CREDIT	
1						1
2						2
3						3
4						4
5						5
6						6
7						7
8						8
9						9
10						10
11						11
12						12
13						13
14						14
15						15
16						16
17						17
18						18
19						19
20						20
21						21
22						22
23						23
24						24
25						25
26						26
27						27
28						28
29						29
30						30
31						31
32						32
33						33

Name ______________________________

Comprehensive Problem 1 (Continued)

JOURNAL

PAGE 3

DATE		DESCRIPTION	POST. REF.	DEBIT	CREDIT

Comprehensive Problem 1 (Continued)

JOURNAL

PAGE 4

DATE		DESCRIPTION	POST. REF.	DEBIT	CREDIT

Name ______________________________

Comprehensive Problem 1 (Continued)

2., 9., and 11.

GENERAL LEDGER

ACCOUNT ACCOUNT NO.

DATE		ITEM	POST. REF.	DEBIT	CREDIT	BALANCE	
						DEBIT	CREDIT

ACCOUNT ACCOUNT NO.

DATE		ITEM	POST. REF.	DEBIT	CREDIT	BALANCE	
						DEBIT	CREDIT

Comprehensive Problem 1 (Continued)

ACCOUNT ACCOUNT NO.

DATE	ITEM	POST. REF.	DEBIT	CREDIT	BALANCE DEBIT	BALANCE CREDIT

ACCOUNT ACCOUNT NO.

DATE	ITEM	POST. REF.	DEBIT	CREDIT	BALANCE DEBIT	BALANCE CREDIT

ACCOUNT ACCOUNT NO.

DATE	ITEM	POST. REF.	DEBIT	CREDIT	BALANCE DEBIT	BALANCE CREDIT

Comprehensive Problem 1 (Continued)

ACCOUNT ACCOUNT NO.

DATE	ITEM	POST. REF.	DEBIT	CREDIT	BALANCE	
					DEBIT	CREDIT

ACCOUNT ACCOUNT NO.

DATE	ITEM	POST. REF.	DEBIT	CREDIT	BALANCE	
					DEBIT	CREDIT

ACCOUNT ACCOUNT NO.

DATE	ITEM	POST. REF.	DEBIT	CREDIT	BALANCE	
					DEBIT	CREDIT

ACCOUNT ACCOUNT NO.

DATE	ITEM	POST. REF.	DEBIT	CREDIT	BALANCE	
					DEBIT	CREDIT

Comprehensive Problem 1 (Continued)

ACCOUNT ACCOUNT NO.

DATE		ITEM	POST. REF.	DEBIT	CREDIT	BALANCE	
						DEBIT	CREDIT

ACCOUNT ACCOUNT NO.

DATE		ITEM	POST. REF.	DEBIT	CREDIT	BALANCE	
						DEBIT	CREDIT

ACCOUNT ACCOUNT NO.

DATE		ITEM	POST. REF.	DEBIT	CREDIT	BALANCE	
						DEBIT	CREDIT

ACCOUNT ACCOUNT NO.

DATE		ITEM	POST. REF.	DEBIT	CREDIT	BALANCE	
						DEBIT	CREDIT

Comprehensive Problem 1 (Continued)

ACCOUNT ACCOUNT NO.

DATE	ITEM	POST. REF.	DEBIT	CREDIT	BALANCE	
					DEBIT	CREDIT

ACCOUNT ACCOUNT NO.

DATE	ITEM	POST. REF.	DEBIT	CREDIT	BALANCE	
					DEBIT	CREDIT

ACCOUNT ACCOUNT NO.

DATE	ITEM	POST. REF.	DEBIT	CREDIT	BALANCE	
					DEBIT	CREDIT

ACCOUNT ACCOUNT NO.

DATE	ITEM	POST. REF.	DEBIT	CREDIT	BALANCE	
					DEBIT	CREDIT

Comprehensive Problem 1 (Continued)

ACCOUNT ACCOUNT NO.

DATE		ITEM	POST. REF.	DEBIT	CREDIT	BALANCE	
						DEBIT	CREDIT

ACCOUNT ACCOUNT NO.

DATE		ITEM	POST. REF.	DEBIT	CREDIT	BALANCE	
						DEBIT	CREDIT

ACCOUNT ACCOUNT NO.

DATE		ITEM	POST. REF.	DEBIT	CREDIT	BALANCE	
						DEBIT	CREDIT

ACCOUNT ACCOUNT NO.

DATE		ITEM	POST. REF.	DEBIT	CREDIT	BALANCE	
						DEBIT	CREDIT

Comprehensive Problem 1 (Continued)

3. and 4.: See pages 120–121.

5.

6.

Comprehensive Problem 1 (Continued)

3. and 4.

	ACCOUNT TITLE	ACCT. NO.	TRIAL BALANCE		ADJUSTMENTS		
			DEBIT	CREDIT	DEBIT	CREDIT	
1							1
2							2
3							3
4							4
5							5
6							6
7							7
8							8
9							9
10							10
11							11
12							12
13							13
14							14
15							15
16							16
17							17
18							18
19							19
20							20
21							21
22							22
23							23
24							24
25							25
26							26
27							27
28							28
29							29
30							30
31							31

Comprehensive Problem 1 (Continued)

	ADJUSTED TRIAL BALANCE		INCOME STATEMENT		BALANCE SHEET	
	DEBIT	CREDIT	DEBIT	CREDIT	DEBIT	CREDIT

Comprehensive Problem 1 (Continued)

7.

Comprehensive Problem 1 (Continued)

8.

JOURNAL PAGE 5

DATE		DESCRIPTION	POST. REF.	DEBIT	CREDIT

Comprehensive Problem 1 (Continued)

10.

JOURNAL PAGE 6

DATE		DESCRIPTION	POST. REF.	DEBIT	CREDIT

Comprehensive Problem 1 (Concluded)

12.

ACCOUNT	ACCT NO.	DEBIT BALANCE	CREDIT BALANCE

Name ______________________________

Exercise 7A1 or 7B1

Cash Basis	Modified Cash Basis	Accrual Basis

Exercise 7A2 or 7B2

COMBINATION JOURNAL

PAGE 1

	DATE	CASH		DESCRIPTION	POST. REF.	GENERAL		FEES CREDIT	SALARY EXPENSE DEBIT	
		DEBIT	CREDIT			DEBIT	CREDIT			
1										1
2										2
3										3
4										4
5										5
6										6
7										7
8										8
9										9
10										10
11										11
12										12
13										13
14										14
15										15
16										16
17										17
18										18
19										19
20										20
21										21
22										22
23										23
24										24
25										25
26										26
27										27
28										28

Exercise 7A3 or 7B3

COMBINATION JOURNAL PAGE 1

	DATE	CASH DEBIT	CASH CREDIT	DESCRIPTION	POST. REF.	GENERAL DEBIT	GENERAL CREDIT	FEES CREDIT	SALARY EXPENSE DEBIT	
1										1
2										2
3										3
4										4
5										5
6										6
7										7
8										8
9										9
10										10
11										11
12										12
13										13
14										14
15										15
16										16
17										17
18										18
19										19
20										20

Proving the Combination Journal:

Problem 7A1 or 7B1

1. and 2.

COMBINATION JOURNAL

PAGE *1*

	DATE	CASH		DESCRIPTION	POST. REF.	GENERAL		FEES CREDIT	SALARY EXPENSE DEBIT		
		DEBIT	CREDIT			DEBIT	CREDIT				
1											1
2											2
3											3
4											4
5											5
6											6
7											7
8											8
9											9
10											10
11											11
12											12
13											13
14											14
15											15
16											16
17											17
18											18
19											19
20											20
21											21
22											22
23											23
24											24
25											25
26											26
27											27

Problem 7A1 or 7B1 (Continued)

2.

GENERAL LEDGER

ACCOUNT ACCOUNT NO.

DATE	ITEM	POST. REF.	DEBIT	CREDIT	BALANCE DEBIT	BALANCE CREDIT

ACCOUNT ACCOUNT NO.

DATE	ITEM	POST. REF.	DEBIT	CREDIT	BALANCE DEBIT	BALANCE CREDIT

ACCOUNT ACCOUNT NO.

DATE	ITEM	POST. REF.	DEBIT	CREDIT	BALANCE DEBIT	BALANCE CREDIT

ACCOUNT ACCOUNT NO.

DATE	ITEM	POST. REF.	DEBIT	CREDIT	BALANCE DEBIT	BALANCE CREDIT

Problem 7A1 or 7B1 (Continued)

ACCOUNT ACCOUNT NO.

DATE		ITEM	POST. REF.	DEBIT	CREDIT	BALANCE	
						DEBIT	CREDIT

ACCOUNT ACCOUNT NO.

DATE		ITEM	POST. REF.	DEBIT	CREDIT	BALANCE	
						DEBIT	CREDIT

ACCOUNT ACCOUNT NO.

DATE		ITEM	POST. REF.	DEBIT	CREDIT	BALANCE	
						DEBIT	CREDIT

ACCOUNT ACCOUNT NO.

DATE		ITEM	POST. REF.	DEBIT	CREDIT	BALANCE	
						DEBIT	CREDIT

ACCOUNT ACCOUNT NO.

DATE		ITEM	POST. REF.	DEBIT	CREDIT	BALANCE	
						DEBIT	CREDIT

Name ______________________________

Problem 7A1 or 7B1 (Continued)

ACCOUNT ACCOUNT NO.

DATE		ITEM	POST. REF.	DEBIT	CREDIT	BALANCE	
						DEBIT	CREDIT

ACCOUNT ACCOUNT NO.

DATE		ITEM	POST. REF.	DEBIT	CREDIT	BALANCE	
						DEBIT	CREDIT

ACCOUNT ACCOUNT NO.

DATE		ITEM	POST. REF.	DEBIT	CREDIT	BALANCE	
						DEBIT	CREDIT

ACCOUNT ACCOUNT NO.

DATE		ITEM	POST. REF.	DEBIT	CREDIT	BALANCE	
						DEBIT	CREDIT

ACCOUNT ACCOUNT NO.

DATE		ITEM	POST. REF.	DEBIT	CREDIT	BALANCE	
						DEBIT	CREDIT

Problem 7A1 or 7B1 (Continued)

3. **Cash Balance:**

4. **Proving the Combination Journal:**

5.

ACCOUNT	ACCT NO.	DEBIT BALANCE	CREDIT BALANCE

Problem 7A1 or 7B1 (Continued)

Problem 7A1 or 7B1 (Concluded)

Problem 7A2 or 7B2

1. and 2.

COMBINATION JOURNAL

PAGE 5

DATE		CASH DEBIT	CASH CREDIT	DESCRIPTION	POST. REF.	GENERAL DEBIT	GENERAL CREDIT	FEES CREDIT	SALARY EXPENSE DEBIT	Advertising exp Debit
NOV	1		300 00	Rent expense	511	300 00				
	2			Tailoring supplies	121	150 00				
				Account payable	211		150 00			
	3			Tailoring equip	141	3000 00				
				Account payable	211		3000 00			
	5	400 00						400 00		
	8		13 00							13 00
	9		28 00	Telephone expense	533	28 00				
	10		21 00	Electricity expense	555	21 00				
	12	200 00						200 00		
	15	600 00	362 00 400 00						400 00	
	16		100 00	Account payable	211	100 00				
	17		12 00	Miscellenous exp	588	12 00				
	19	450						450 00		
	21		500	Prepaid insurance	131	500 00				
	23	300 00						300 00		
	24		13 00							13 00
	26		12 00	Mis expense	588	12 00				
	29	600 00						600 00		
		1950 00	1399 00			4123 00	3150 00	1950 00	400 00	26 00
		(101)	(101)			(✓)	(✓)	(411)	(522)	(566)

Problem 7A2 or 7B2 (Continued)

2.

GENERAL LEDGER

ACCOUNT Cash ACCOUNT NO. 101

DATE		ITEM	POST. REF.	DEBIT	CREDIT	BALANCE DEBIT	BALANCE CREDIT
19 Nov	1	Balance	✓			6 2 1 1 50	
	30		CJ5	1 9 5 0 00		8 1 6 1 50	
	30		CJ5		1 3 9 0 00	6 7 6 2 50	

ACCOUNT Office supplies ACCOUNT NO. 111

DATE		ITEM	POST. REF.	DEBIT	CREDIT	BALANCE DEBIT	BALANCE CREDIT
19 Nov	1	Balance	✓			4 8 4 50	
	30	Adjusting	CJ6		2 0 0 00	2 8 4 50	

ACCOUNT Tailoring supplies ACCOUNT NO. 121

DATE		ITEM	POST. REF.	DEBIT	CREDIT	BALANCE DEBIT	BALANCE CREDIT
19 Nov	1	Balance	✓			1 0 0 0 00	
	2		CJ5	1 5 0		1 1 5 0 00	
	30	Adjusting	CJ6		7 0 0 00	4 5 0 00	

ACCOUNT Pre-paid insurance ACCOUNT NO. 131

DATE		ITEM	POST. REF.	DEBIT	CREDIT	BALANCE DEBIT	BALANCE CREDIT
	1	Balance	✓			1 0 0 00	
	21		CJ5	5 0 0 00		6 0 0 00	
	30	Adj	CJ6		1 5 0 00	4 5 0 00	

Problem 7A2 or 7B2 (Continued)

ACCOUNT Tailoring Equip ACCOUNT NO. 141

DATE		ITEM	POST. REF.	DEBIT	CREDIT	BALANCE DEBIT	BALANCE CREDIT
Nov	1	Bal	✓			3500 00	
	3		CJ5	3300 00		6800 00	

ACCOUNT Accum. Depr – Tail Equip ACCOUNT NO. 141.1

DATE		ITEM	POST. REF.	DEBIT	CREDIT	BALANCE DEBIT	BALANCE CREDIT
19 Nov		Bal	✓				800 00
		Adj	CJ6		300 00		1100 00

ACCOUNT Accounts payable ACCOUNT NO. 211

DATE		ITEM	POST. REF.	DEBIT	CREDIT	BALANCE DEBIT	BALANCE CREDIT
19 Nov		Bal	✓				4125 00
			CJ5		150 00		4275 00
			CJ5		3000 00		7275 00
			CJ5	100			7175 00

ACCOUNT Sue – Raylin, Capital ACCOUNT NO. 311

DATE		ITEM	POST. REF.	DEBIT	CREDIT	BALANCE DEBIT	BALANCE CREDIT
	1	Bal	✓				5430 00
	30	Closing	CJ6		1842 00		7272 00
	30	Closing	CJ6	800 00			6472 00

Problem 7A2 or 7B2 (Continued)

ACCOUNT Sue Raylai Drawing ACCOUNT NO. 312

DATE		ITEM	POST. REF.	DEBIT	CREDIT	BALANCE DEBIT	BALANCE CREDIT
Nov 19—	1	Bal	✓			800	
	30	Closing	CJ6		800	—	—

ACCOUNT Income Summary ACCOUNT NO. 331

DATE		ITEM	POST. REF.	DEBIT	CREDIT	BALANCE DEBIT	BALANCE CREDIT
Nov 19—	30	Closing	CJ6		5550 w		5550 w
	"	"	"	3708 w			1842 w
	"	"	"	1842 w		—	—

ACCOUNT Tailoring fee ACCOUNT NO. 411

DATE		ITEM	POST. REF.	DEBIT	CREDIT	BALANCE DEBIT	BALANCE CREDIT
Nov 19—	1		✓				3600 w
	30		CJ5		1950 w		5550 w
	30		CJ5	5550 w	—		—

ACCOUNT Rent exp ACCOUNT NO. 511

DATE		ITEM	POST. REF.	DEBIT	CREDIT	BALANCE DEBIT	BALANCE CREDIT
Nov 19—	1	Bal	✓			600 w	
	11		CJ5	300 w		900 w	
	30	Closing	CJ5		900 w	—	—

Problem 7A2 or 7B2 (Continued)

ACCOUNT Salary exp ACCOUNT NO. 522

DATE		ITEM	POST. REF.	DEBIT	CREDIT	BALANCE DEBIT	BALANCE CREDIT
19 Nov	1	Bal	✓			800 00	
	30		CJ5	400 00		1200 00	
	30	closing	CJ6		1200 00	—	—

ACCOUNT Telep exp ACCOUNT NO. 533

DATE		ITEM	POST. REF.	DEBIT	CREDIT	BALANCE DEBIT	BALANCE CREDIT
19 Nov	1	Bal	✓			60 00	
	9		CJ5	28 00		88 00	
	30	closing	CJ6		88 00	—	—

ACCOUNT T. *Supplies Expense* ACCOUNT NO. *541*

DATE		ITEM	POST. REF.	DEBIT	CREDIT	BALANCE DEBIT	BALANCE CREDIT
19 Nov	30	Adj	CJ6	700 00		700 00	
	30	closing	CJ6		700 00	—	—

ACCOUNT *Office Supplies Expense* ACCOUNT NO. *542*

DATE		ITEM	POST. REF.	DEBIT	CREDIT	BALANCE DEBIT	BALANCE CREDIT
19 Nov	30	Adj	CJ6	200 00		200	
	30	closing	CJ6		200 00	—	—

Problem 7A2 or 7B2 (Continued)

ACCOUNT *Insurance Expense* ACCOUNT NO. *543*

DATE		ITEM	POST. REF.	DEBIT	CREDIT	BALANCE DEBIT	BALANCE CREDIT
Nov	30	Adj	CJ6	150 00		150 00	
	30	clos	CJ6		150 00	—	—

ACCOUNT *Depreciation Expense* ACCOUNT NO. *544*

DATE		ITEM	POST. REF.	DEBIT	CREDIT	BALANCE DEBIT	BALANCE CREDIT
	30	Adj	CJ6	300 00		300	
	31	closing	CJ6		300 00	—	—

ACCOUNT Elec exp ACCOUNT NO. 555

DATE		ITEM	POST. REF.	DEBIT	CREDIT	BALANCE DEBIT	BALANCE CREDIT
	1	Bal	✓			44 00	
	10		CJ5	21 00		65 00	
	30	closing	CJ5		65 00	—	—

ACCOUNT Advertising exp ACCOUNT NO. 566

DATE		ITEM	POST. REF.	DEBIT	CREDIT	BALANCE DEBIT	BALANCE CREDIT
	1	Bal	✓			33 00	
	30		CJ5	26 00		59 00	
	30	closing	CJ6		59 00	—	—

Problem 7A2 or 7B2 (Continued)

ACCOUNT Mis exp ACCOUNT NO. 588

DATE		ITEM	POST. REF.	DEBIT	CREDIT	BALANCE DEBIT	BALANCE CREDIT
	1	Bal	✓			22 00	
	17		CJ5	12 00		34 00	
	26		CJ5	12 00		46 00	
	30	closing	J6		46 00	—	—

3. **Cash Balance:** Jan 13:

Beginning Balance	$6,211.59
cash Debits	600.00
	$6,811.50
Less: cash credits	362.00
Balance	$6,449.59

4. **Proving the Combination Journal:**

Debits columns:		Credits columns	
Cash	$1,950	cash	1,399
General	4,230	general	3,150
Salary exp	400	Fee	1,950
Adv. exp	26		
	$6,499		6,499

Problem 7A2 or 7B2 (Continued)

5.

Sue
Work
For Three Months

ACCOUNT TITLE	ACCT. NO.	TRIAL BALANCE DEBIT	TRIAL BALANCE CREDIT	ADJUSTMENTS DEBIT	ADJUSTMENTS CREDIT
Cash	101	6762 50			
office supplies	111	464 50			b 200 00
Tail sup	121	1150 00			a 700 00
pre paid ins	131	600 00			c 150 00
Tail equip	141	6800 00			
Acc Depr – Tail eq	141.1		800 00		d 300 00
Ac. payable	211		7175 00		
Sue R. capital	311		5430 00		
" Drawing	312	800 00			
Tailoring fee	411		5550 00		
Rent expense	511	900 00			
salary expense	522	1200 00			
Telephone exp.	533	88 00			
Ele. exp	555	65 00			
Ad. exp	566	59 00			
Mis. exp	588	48 00			
		18955 00	18955 00		
Tail sup ex	541			a 700 00	
off sup exp	542			b 200 00	
insurance exp	543			c 150 00	
Depr. exp	544			d 300 00	
				1350 00	1350 00
Net income					

Name ______________________________

Problem 7A2 or 7B2 (Continued)

Reylá
Sheet
ended Nov 30,

	ADJUSTED TRIAL BALANCE		INCOME STATEMENT		BALANCE SHEET		
	DEBIT	CREDIT	DEBIT	CREDIT	DEBIT	CREDIT	
1	6762 50				6762 50		1
2	284 50				284 —		2
3	450 —				450 —		3
4	450 —				450 —		4
5	6880 —				6880		5
6		1100 —				1100	6
7		7175 —				7175 —	7
8		5430 —				5430 —	8
9	800				800 —		9
10		5550 —		5550 —			10
11	900 —		900 —				11
12	1200 —		1200 —				12
13	88 —		88 —				13
14	65 —		65 —				14
15	59 —		59 —				15
16	46 —		46 —				16
17							17
18	700 —		700 —				18
19	200 —		240 —				19
20	150 —		150 —				20
21	300 —		300 —				21
22	19255 —		19255 —	5550 —	1554 —	13705 —	22
23			18420 —			1842 —	23
24			5550 —	555 —		15547 —	24
25							25
26							26
27							27
28							28
29							29
30							30

Problem 7A2 or 7B2 (Continued)

COMBINATION JOURNAL PAGE 6

	DATE	CASH DEBIT	CASH CREDIT	DESCRIPTION	POST. REF.	GENERAL DEBIT	GENERAL CREDIT	FEES CREDIT	SALARY EXPENSE DEBIT		
				Adjusting entries							
1	Nov 30			Tail sup exp	541	700					1
2					121		700	[illegible]			2
3	30			Tail sup	542	200					3
4				off sup ex	111		200				4
5	30			off sup	543	150					5
6				insure exp	131		150				6
7				pre-paid ins	544	300					7
8	30			Dep. exp	141.1		300				8
9				Acc. Dep. Tail eq							9
10											10
11				closing entries							11
12	30				411	5550					12
13					331		5550				13
14	30				331	3708					14
15					511		900				15
16					522		1200				16
17					53		48				17
18					541		700				18
19					542		200				19
20					543		150				20
21					544		300				21
22					553		65				22
23					566		59				23
24					588		46				24
25	30				331	1842					25
26					311						26
27	30				311	800					27
28					312		800				28

Name ______________________________

Problem 7A2 or 7B2 (Continued)

6.

Sue Raylor
Income Sheet
For three months

Revenue		$5550
Tailor fee		
Expenses:		
Salary exp	1200	
Rent exp	900	
Tail sup exp	700	
Dep exp	300	
Off sup exp	200	
Ins exp	150	
Tel exp	88	
Ele exp	65	
Adve exp	54	
Mis exp	46	
Total exp		3708
Net Income		1842

Problem 7A2 or 7B2 (Concluded)

Mastery Problem

1.

COMBINATION JOURNAL PAGE 1

	DATE	CASH DEBIT	CASH CREDIT	DESCRIPTION	POST. REF.	GENERAL DEBIT	GENERAL CREDIT	REGISTRATION FEES CREDIT	WAGE EXPENSE DEBIT	FOOD SUPPLIES DEBIT	
1											1
2											2
3											3
4											4
5											5
6											6
7											7
8											8
9											9
10											10
11											11
12											12
13											13
14											14
15											15
16											16
17											17
18											18
19											19
20											20
21											21
22											22
23											23
24											24
25											25
26											26
27											27

Mastery Problem (Continued)

2. **Proving the Combination Journal:**

3.

GENERAL LEDGER

ACCOUNT *Cash* ACCOUNT NO. *111*

DATE		ITEM	POST. REF.	DEBIT	CREDIT	BALANCE	
						DEBIT	CREDIT

ACCOUNT *Office Supplies* ACCOUNT NO. *152*

DATE		ITEM	POST. REF.	DEBIT	CREDIT	BALANCE	
						DEBIT	CREDIT

ACCOUNT *Food Supplies* ACCOUNT NO. *154*

DATE		ITEM	POST. REF.	DEBIT	CREDIT	BALANCE	
						DEBIT	CREDIT

Mastery Problem (Continued)

ACCOUNT *Tennis Facilities* ACCOUNT NO. *183*

DATE	ITEM	POST. REF.	DEBIT	CREDIT	BALANCE DEBIT	BALANCE CREDIT

ACCOUNT *Accounts Payable* ACCOUNT NO. *218*

DATE	ITEM	POST. REF.	DEBIT	CREDIT	BALANCE DEBIT	BALANCE CREDIT

ACCOUNT *James Goodbody, Capital* ACCOUNT NO. *311*

DATE	ITEM	POST. REF.	DEBIT	CREDIT	BALANCE DEBIT	BALANCE CREDIT

ACCOUNT *James Goodbody, Drawing* ACCOUNT NO. *312*

DATE	ITEM	POST. REF.	DEBIT	CREDIT	BALANCE DEBIT	BALANCE CREDIT

Mastery Problem (Continued)

ACCOUNT *Registration Fees* ACCOUNT NO. *411*

DATE		ITEM	POST. REF.	DEBIT	CREDIT	BALANCE DEBIT	BALANCE CREDIT

ACCOUNT *Wage Expense* ACCOUNT NO. *542*

DATE		ITEM	POST. REF.	DEBIT	CREDIT	BALANCE DEBIT	BALANCE CREDIT

ACCOUNT *Telephone Expense* ACCOUNT NO. *545*

DATE		ITEM	POST. REF.	DEBIT	CREDIT	BALANCE DEBIT	BALANCE CREDIT

ACCOUNT *Utility Expense* ACCOUNT NO. *549*

DATE		ITEM	POST. REF.	DEBIT	CREDIT	BALANCE DEBIT	BALANCE CREDIT

ACCOUNT *Postage Expense* ACCOUNT NO. *564*

DATE		ITEM	POST. REF.	DEBIT	CREDIT	BALANCE DEBIT	BALANCE CREDIT

Mastery Problem (Concluded)

4.

ACCOUNT	ACCT NO.	DEBIT BALANCE	CREDIT BALANCE

Exercise 8A1 or 8B1

1. c
2. e
3. a
4. d
5. f
6. g
7. b

Exercise 8A2 or 8A3

DEPOSIT TICKET 63-1209/631

WIZARD BANK
3711 Buena Vista Dr.
Orlando, FL 32811-1314

DATE ______________________ 19 - -

CHECKS AND OTHER ITEMS ARE RECEIVED FOR DEPOSIT SUBJECT TO THE TERMS AND CONDITIONS OF THIS FINANCIAL INSTITUTION'S ACCOUNT AGREEMENT.

SIGN HERE ONLY IF CASH RECEIVED FROM DEPOSIT

⑆063112094

CURRENCY		334	92
COIN		26	00
CHECKS	4-11	311	00
	80-322	105	00
	3-9	38	00
TOTAL FROM OTHER SIDE			
SUB-TOTAL		817	00
LESS CASH RECEIVED			
TOTAL DEPOSIT		817	00

Exercise 8A3 or 8B3

NO.1

DATE Jan 15 19 - -
TO J. M Supply
FOR offi. supp
ACCT. ______

	DOLLARS	CENTS
BAL. BRO'T FOR'D	2,841	50
AMT. DEPOSITED	817	00
TOTAL	3,658	50
AMT. THIS CHECK	150	00
BAL. CAR'D FOR'D	3,508	50

NO.1 63-1209/631

______________ 19 ____

PAY TO THE ORDER OF ______________________ $ 150

one hundred fifty 00/100 ______ DOLLARS

FOR CLASSROOM USE ONLY

WIZARD BANK

BY student's sign

⑆063112094

Exercise 8A4 or 8B4

	Ending Bank Balance	Ending Check-Book Balance
a.	+	
b.		+
c.		−
d.	−	
e.		−
f.		+
g.		+

Exercise 8A5 or 8B5

JOURNAL PAGE

	DATE		DESCRIPTION	POST. REF.	DEBIT	CREDIT	
1	Sep	30	Acc. payable		1 00		1
2			Cash			1 00	2
3			Error in check no. 39.				3
4							4
5		30	Account receivable		400 00		5
6			cash			400 00	6
7			NSF check				7
8							8
9		30	Miscellaneous expense		8 30		9
10			cash			8 30	10
11			Banks service fee				11
12							12
13							13
14							14
15							15
16							16
17							17
18							18
19							19
20							20
21							21
22							22
23							23

Name Zoheda

Exercise 8A6 or 8B6

JOURNAL PAGE

DATE		DESCRIPTION	POST. REF.	DEBIT	CREDIT
1		Petty Cash		150	
		cash			150
		To establish petty cash fund			
	31	Telephones exp		3.50	
		Auto exp		11 00	
		J Adams Drawing		50 00	
		Postage exp		8 50	
		Charitable contribution exp		10 00	
		Miscellaneous exp		28 00	
		cash			111 00
		Replenish petty cash fund			

Exercise 8A7 or 8B7

JOURNAL

PAGE

DATE		DESCRIPTION	POST. REF.	DEBIT	CREDIT
Apr	2	Cash		266 50	
		Cash short and over		2 00	
		Revenue			268 50
	9	Cash		233 50	
		cash short & over		4 25	
		Revenue			237 50
	16	Cash		311 00	
		cash Short & over			1 75
		Revenue			309 00
	23	Cash		224	
		cash Short & over		2 50	
		Revenue			226 00
	30	Cash		322 00	
		cash short & ove			4 00
		Revenue			318 00

Name Zaheda

Problem 8A1 or 8B1

1.

Bank Reconcilliation
Oct 30 19

Bank Statement Balance, oct 30		2856 00
Add Deposit in Transit 10/28	$300 00	
10/29	280 00	580 00
Sub Total		3436 00
Deduct-outstanding ch NO 2826	$ 58 00	
NO 2829	122 00	
NO 2833	360 00	540 00
Adjusted Bank Balance		$2896 00
Book Balance, oct 30		3184 00
Add Che Error (#2818)		10 00
		3194 00
Deduct Bank Service Charg	$ 20 00	
" NSF Che	278 00	298 00
Adj Book Balance		$ 2896 00

2.

JOURNAL PAGE

	DATE		DESCRIPTION	POST. REF.	DEBIT	CREDIT	
1	Oct	30	Cash		10 00		1
2			acount payable			10 00	2
3			Error on check# 2818				3
4							4
5		30	Miscellaneous exp		20 00		5
6			Cash			20 00	6
7			Bank service charge				7
8							8
9		30	Account Receivable		278 00		9
10			cash			278 00	10
11			NSF check				11
12							12
13							13

Problem 8A2 or 8B2

1. and 3.

JOURNAL

PAGE

	DATE		DESCRIPTION	POST. REF.	DEBIT	CREDIT	
1	May	1	Petty cash		150 00		1
2			Cash			150 00	2
3			To establish petty cash fund				3
4							4
5		31	Supplies exp		11 00		5
6			Postage exp		7 00		6
7			Charitable contribution exp		40 00		7
8			Telephone exp		5 00		8
9			Travel exp		28 00		9
10			Miscellaneous exp		22 00		10
11			J. Adams, Drawing		25 00		11
12			Replenish cash fund			138 00	12

Problem 8A2 or 8B2 (Concluded)

2. and 3.

PETTY CASH PAYMENTS FOR THE MONTH OF May 19 PAGE

	DAY	DESCRIPTION	VOU. NO.	TOTAL AMOUNT	DISTRIBUTION OF DEBITS: SUPPLIES EXP.	POSTAGE EXP.	CHAR. CON. EXP.	TELEPHONE EXP.	TRAVEL EXP.	MISC. EXP.	ACCOUNT	AMOUNT	
1	1	establish fund $150											1
2	1	Postage	1	3 50		3 50							2
3	3	Supplies	2	11 00	11 00								3
4	4	auto repair	3	22 00						22 00			4
5	7	J. Adams, drawing	4	25 00							J Adams Drawing	25 00	5
6	11	Donation	5	10 00			10 00						6
7	15	Travel exp	6	28 00					28 00				7
8	22	postage	7	3 50		3 50							8
9	26	Telephone call	8	5 00				5 00					9
10	30	Donation	9	30 00			30 00						10
11				138 00	11 00	7 00	40 00	5 00	28 00	22 00		25 00	11
12	31	Bal $12.00											12
13		Replenished 138.00											13
14		Total 150.00											14
15													15
16													16
17													17
18													18
19													19
20													20

Problem 8A3 or 8B3

1.

JOURNAL

PAGE 8

DATE		DESCRIPTION	POST. REF.	DEBIT	CREDIT
July	2	Cash		287 00	
		Cash Short & Over		2 50	
		Revenue			289 00
	9	Cash		311 50	
		Revenue			311 50
	16	Cash		308 00	
		Cash Sh & Over			2 50
		Revenue			306 00
	23	Cash		315 00	
		Cash Short & Over		2 50	
		Revenue			317 00
	30	Cash		299 50	
		Cash Short & Over			3 50
		Revenue			296 00

2. and 3.

ACCOUNT ACCOUNT NO.

DATE		ITEM	POST. REF.	DEBIT	CREDIT	BALANCE DEBIT	BALANCE CREDIT
July	2		J8	2 50		2 50	
	16		J8		2 50	—	—
	23		J8	2 50		2 50	
	30		J8		3 50		1 00

Revenue

Mastery Problem

1.

JOURNAL

PAGE

DATE		DESCRIPTION	POST. REF.	DEBIT	CREDIT

Mastery Problem (Continued)

JOURNAL

PAGE

	DATE		DESCRIPTION	POST. REF.	DEBIT	CREDIT	
1							1
2							2
3							3
4							4
5							5
6							6
7							7
8							8
9							9
10							10
11							11
12							12
13							13
14							14
15							15
16							16
17							17
18							18
19							19
20							20
21							21
22							22
23							23
24							24
25							25
26							26
27							27
28							28
29							29
30							30
31							31
32							32

Mastery Problem (Continued)

1.

PETTY CASH PAYMENTS FOR THE MONTH OF 19 PAGE

	DAY	DESCRIPTION	VOU. NO.	TOTAL AMOUNT	DISTRIBUTION OF DEBITS								
					TRUCK EXP.	POSTAGE EXP.	CHAR. CON. EXP.	TELEPHONE EXP.	ADVER. EXP.	MISC. EXP.	ACCOUNT	AMOUNT	
1													1
2													2
3													3
4													4
5													5
6													6
7													7
8													8
9													9
10													10
11													11
12													12
13													13
14													14
15													15
16													16
17													17
18													18
19													19
20													20

Mastery Problem (Concluded)

2.

Exercise 9A1 or 9B1

a. 40 hours at straight time × 10.00 per hour — 400.00
b. 6.00 hours overtime × 15.00 per hour — 90.00
c. Total gross wages — 490.00
d. Federal income tax withholding (from tax tables in Figure 9-4) — 49.00
e. FICA withholding at 7.5 percent — 36.75
f. Total withholding — 75.75
g. Net pay — 414.25

Exercise 9A2 or 9B2

Regular hours h 40 x 15 = $600
overtime 1.5 h 2 x 22.50 = 45
overtime 2.00 h 5 x 30 = 150
Total $795

Exercise 9A3 or 9B3

a.
2,600 x 12 = 31,200 Annual pay
31,200 / 52 = 600 pay / w
600 / 40 = $15 / h
15 x 1.5 = 22.50 / h overtime

b.
regular pay = 40 x 15 = 600.00
over Time 5 x 22.50 = 112.50
Total 712.50

Exercise 9A4 or 9B4

	Amount of Withholding	weekly earnings	N of allowances
a.	327.90	2	26
b.	410.00	1	46
c.	438.16	5	24
d.	518.25	0	67
e.	603.90	6	43

Exercise 9A5 or 9B5

Year-to Date Earnings	Amount not Subject to FICA	Amount Subject to FICA	FICA Tax Withheld
23,200	none	1,200	90
58,200	3,200	1,000	75
57,125	2,125	1,800	135
60,600	4,600	none	none

Exercise 9A6 or 9B6

FICA Tax = 7,300 x .075 = 547.50

JOURNAL PAGE

	DATE		DESCRIPTION	POST. REF.	DEBIT	CREDIT	
1	Dec	31	Wages + salary expense		8700 00		1
2			Employee tax payable			920 00	2
3			FICA Taxable 7.5%			547.50	3
4			united way contribution			200 00	4
5			Cash			7032 50	5
6							6
7							7
8							8
9							9

Exercise 9A7 or 9B7

JOURNAL PAGE

	DATE		DESCRIPTION	POST. REF.	DEBIT	CREDIT	
1	Ap	15	Wages + salary exp		6242 00		1
2			Federal Tax			593 00	2
3			FICA Tax			468 15	3
4			Pension plan			90 00	4
5			Health insurance			225 00	5
6			united way			100 00	6
7			cash			4765 85	7
8							8
9							9

Name zahedi

Problem 9A1 or 9B1

1.

Regular pay = 40 x 8.50	340.00	
overtime 8 x 12.75	102.00	
Gross pay	442.00	
Deduction		
Employee Income Tax		32.00
FICA tax $442 x .075		33.15
Health insurance		85.00
credit union contribution		125.00
united way contribution		10.00
Total		285.15
Net pay		156.85

2.

JOURNAL PAGE

	DATE		DESCRIPTION	POST. REF.	DEBIT	CREDIT	
1							1
2							2
3							3
4							4
5							5
6							6
7							7
8							8
9							9
10							10
11							11
12							12
13							13
14							14
15							15

Problem 9A2 or 9B2

1.

PAYROLL REGISTER

	NAME	EMPLOYEE NO.	ALLOW-ANCES	MARITAL STATUS	EARNINGS				TAXABLE EARNINGS	
					REGULAR	OVER-TIME	TOTAL	CUMULATIVE TOTAL	UNEMPLOY COMP.	FICA
1										
2										
3										
4										
5										
6										
7										
8										
9										
10										
11										
12										

Name ____________________

Problem 9A2 or 9B2 (Concluded)

FOR PERIOD ENDED 19--

DEDUCTIONS							NET PAY	CK. NO.	
FEDERAL INC. TAX	FICA TAX	HEALTH INS.	CREDIT UNION	UNITED WAY	OTHER	TOTAL			
									1
									2
									3
									4
									5
									6
									7
									8
									9
									10
									11
									12

2.

JOURNAL PAGE

	DATE	DESCRIPTION	POST. REF.	DEBIT	CREDIT	
1						1
2						2
3						3
4						4
5						5
6						6
7						7
8						8
9						9
10						10
11						11
12						12
13						13
14						14

Problem 9A3 or 9B3

1.

PAYROLL REGISTER March 22, 19

	NAME	EMPLOYEE NO.	ALLOW-ANCES	MARITAL STATUS	EARNINGS				TAXABLE EARNINGS	
					REGULAR	OVER-TIME	TOTAL	CUMULATIVE TOTAL	UNEMPLOY COMP.	FICA
1	Anderson, Loren	1	4	M	440 00	55 00	499 00			499 00
2	Carson, Judy	2	1	M	480 00	00 00	480 00	?		480 00
3	Zliss, Susan	3	3	M	380 00	28 50	408 50			408 50
4	Knox, Wayne	4	1	M	429	— —	429 00			429 00
5	Peters, Jim	5	2	M	420 00	— —	420 00			420 00
6					2149 00	83 50	2236 50			2,236 50
7										
8										
9										
10										
11										
12										

Name ____________________

Problem 9A3 or 9B3 (Concluded)

FOR PERIOD ENDED 19--

	DEDUCTIONS								
FEDERAL INC. TAX	FICA TAX	CITY TAX	LIFE INS.	HEALTH INS.	CREDIT UNION	OTHER	TOTAL	NET PAY	CK. NO.
									1
									2
									3
									4
									5
									6
									7
									8
									9
									10
									11
									12

2.

JOURNAL PAGE

	DATE		DESCRIPTION	POST. REF.	DEBIT	CREDIT	
1	Mar	22	Wages & Salary exp				1
2			FICA Tax				2
3			Employee Incom Tax				3
4			City tax payable				4
5			Life insurance payable				5
6			Health insurance payable				6
7			Credit-union payable				7
8			U.S. Saving Bonds p				8
9			Cash.				9
10							10
11							11
12							12
13							13
14							14

Problem 9A4 or 9B4

EMPLOYEE'S EARNINGS RECORD

19-- PERIOD ENDING	EARNINGS				TAXABLE EARNINGS		DEDUCTIONS	
	REGULAR	OVERTIME	TOTAL	CUMULATIVE TOTAL	UNEMPLOY. COMP.	FICA	FEDERAL INC. TAX	FICA TAX

SEX		DEPARTMENT	OCCUPATION	SOCIAL SECURITY NO.	MARITAL STATUS	EXEMP-TIONS
M	F					

Problem 9A4 or 9B4 (Concluded)

FOR PERIOD ENDED 19--

DEDUCTIONS						NET PAY	
CITY TAX	LIFE INS.	HEALTH INS.	CREDIT UNION	OTHER	TOTAL	CK. NO.	AMOUNT

PAY RATE	DATE OF BIRTH	DATE EMPLOYED	NAME-LAST	FIRST	MIDDLE	EMP. NO.

Mastery Problem

1.

PAYROLL REGISTER

	NAME	EMPLOYEE NO.	ALLOW-ANCES	MARITAL STATUS	EARNINGS				TAXABLE EARNINGS	
					REGULAR	OVER-TIME	TOTAL	CUMULATIVE TOTAL	UNEMPLOY COMP.	FICA
1										
2										
3										
4										
5										
6										
7										
8										
9										
10										
11										
12										
13										
14										
15										
16										

3.

EMPLOYEE'S EARNINGS RECORD

19-- PERIOD ENDING	EARNINGS				TAXABLE EARNINGS		DEDUCTIONS	
	REGULAR	OVERTIME	TOTAL	CUMULATIVE TOTAL	UNEMPLOY. COMP.	FICA	FEDERAL INC. TAX	FICA TAX

SEX		DEPARTMENT	OCCUPATION	SOCIAL SECURITY NO.	MARITAL STATUS	EXEMP-TIONS
M	F					

Mastery Problem (Continued)

FOR PERIOD ENDED 19--

DEDUCTIONS									NET PAY	CK. NO.	
FEDERAL INC. TAX	FICA TAX	STATE INC. TAX	LOCAL INC. TAX	LIFE INS.	HEALTH INS.	CREDIT UNION	OTHER	TOTAL			
											1
											2
											3
											4
											5
											6
											7
											8
											9
											10
											11
											12
											13
											14
											15
											16

FOR PERIOD ENDED *November 25, 19--*

DEDUCTIONS							NET PAY	
STATE INC. TAX	LOCAL INC. TAX	LIFE INS.	HEALTH INS.	CREDIT UNION	OTHER	TOTAL	CK. NO.	AMOUNT

PAY RATE	DATE OF BIRTH	DATE EMPLOYED	NAME-LAST	FIRST	MIDDLE	EMP. NO.

Mastery Problem (Concluded)

2.

JOURNAL

PAGE

DATE		DESCRIPTION	POST. REF.	DEBIT	CREDIT

WEEKLY Payroll Period—Employee MARRIED

And the wages are-		And the number of withholding allowances claimed is—										
At least	But less than	0	1	2	3	4	5	6	7	8	9	10 or more
		The amount of income tax to be withheld shall be—										
$0	$60	$0	$0	$0	$0	$0	$0	$0	$0	$0	$0	$0
60	65	1	0	0	0	0	0	0	0	0	0	0
65	70	1	0	0	0	0	0	0	0	0	0	0
70	75	2	0	0	0	0	0	0	0	0	0	0
75	80	3	0	0	0	0	0	0	0	0	0	0
80	85	4	0	0	0	0	0	0	0	0	0	0
85	90	4	0	0	0	0	0	0	0	0	0	0
90	95	5	0	0	0	0	0	0	0	0	0	0
95	100	6	0	0	0	0	0	0	0	0	0	0
100	105	7	1	0	0	0	0	0	0	0	0	0
105	110	7	2	0	0	0	0	0	0	0	0	0
110	115	8	2	0	0	0	0	0	0	0	0	0
115	120	9	3	0	0	0	0	0	0	0	0	0
120	125	10	4	0	0	0	0	0	0	0	0	0
125	130	10	5	0	0	0	0	0	0	0	0	0
130	135	11	5	0	0	0	0	0	0	0	0	0
135	140	12	6	1	0	0	0	0	0	0	0	0
140	145	13	7	1	0	0	0	0	0	0	0	0
145	150	13	8	2	0	0	0	0	0	0	0	0
150	155	14	8	3	0	0	0	0	0	0	0	0
155	160	15	9	4	0	0	0	0	0	0	0	0
160	165	16	10	4	0	0	0	0	0	0	0	0
165	170	16	11	5	0	0	0	0	0	0	0	0
170	175	17	11	6	0	0	0	0	0	0	0	0
175	180	18	12	7	1	0	0	0	0	0	0	0
180	185	19	13	7	2	0	0	0	0	0	0	0
185	190	19	14	8	2	0	0	0	0	0	0	0
190	195	20	14	9	3	0	0	0	0	0	0	0
195	200	21	15	10	4	0	0	0	0	0	0	0
200	210	22	16	11	5	0	0	0	0	0	0	0
210	220	23	18	12	7	1	0	0	0	0	0	0
220	230	25	19	14	8	2	0	0	0	0	0	0
230	240	26	21	15	10	4	0	0	0	0	0	0
240	250	28	22	17	11	5	0	0	0	0	0	0
250	260	29	24	18	13	7	1	0	0	0	0	0
At least	But less than	0	1	2	3	4	5	6	7	8	9	10 or more
260	270	31	25	20	14	8	3	0	0	0	0	0
270	280	32	27	21	16	10	4	0	0	0	0	0
280	290	34	28	23	17	11	6	0	0	0	0	0
290	300	35	30	24	19	13	7	2	0	0	0	0
300	310	37	31	26	20	14	9	3	0	0	0	0
310	320	38	33	27	22	16	10	5	0	0	0	0
320	330	40	34	29	23	17	12	6	1	0	0	0
330	340	41	36	30	25	19	13	8	2	0	0	0
340	350	43	37	32	26	20	15	9	4	0	0	0
350	360	44	39	33	28	22	16	11	5	0	0	0
360	370	46	40	35	29	23	18	12	7	1	0	0
370	380	47	42	36	31	25	19	14	8	2	0	0
380	390	49	43	38	32	26	21	15	10	4	0	0
390	400	50	45	39	34	28	22	17	11	5	0	0
400	410	52	46	41	35	29	24	18	13	7	1	0
410	420	53	48	42	37	31	25	20	14	8	3	0
420	430	55	49	44	38	32	27	21	16	10	4	0
430	440	56	51	45	40	34	28	23	17	11	6	0
440	450	58	52	47	41	35	30	24	19	13	7	2
450	460	59	54	48	43	37	31	26	20	14	9	3
460	470	61	55	50	44	38	33	27	22	16	10	5
470	480	62	57	51	46	40	34	29	23	17	12	6
480	490	64	58	53	47	41	36	30	25	19	13	8
490	500	65	60	54	49	43	37	32	26	20	15	9
500	510	67	61	56	50	44	39	33	28	22	16	11
510	520	68	63	57	52	46	40	35	29	23	18	12
520	530	70	64	59	53	47	42	36	31	25	19	14
530	540	71	66	60	55	49	43	38	32	26	21	15
540	550	73	67	62	56	50	45	39	34	28	22	17
550	560	74	69	63	58	52	46	41	35	29	24	18
560	570	76	70	65	59	53	48	42	37	31	25	20
570	580	77	72	66	61	55	49	44	38	32	27	21
580	590	79	73	68	62	56	51	45	40	34	28	23
590	600	80	75	69	64	58	52	47	41	35	30	24
600	610	82	76	71	65	59	54	48	43	37	31	26

WEEKLY Payroll Period—Employee MARRIED

And the wages are-		And the number of withholding allowances claimed is—										
At least	But less than	0	1	2	3	4	5	6	7	8	9	10 or more
		The amount of income tax to be withheld shall be—										
$610	$620	$83	$78	$72	$67	$61	$55	$50	$44	$38	$33	$27
620	630	85	79	74	68	62	57	51	46	40	34	29
630	640	87	81	75	70	64	58	53	47	41	36	30
640	650	90	82	77	71	65	60	54	49	43	37	32
650	660	93	84	78	73	67	61	56	50	44	39	33
660	670	95	85	80	74	68	63	57	52	46	40	35
670	680	98	88	81	76	70	64	59	53	47	42	36
680	690	101	91	83	77	71	66	60	55	49	43	38
690	700	104	93	84	79	73	67	62	56	50	45	39
700	710	107	96	86	80	74	69	63	58	52	46	41
710	720	109	99	88	82	76	70	65	59	53	48	42
720	730	112	102	91	83	77	72	66	61	55	49	44
730	740	115	105	94	85	79	73	68	62	56	51	45
740	750	118	107	97	86	80	75	69	64	58	52	47
750	760	121	110	100	89	82	76	71	65	59	54	48
760	770	123	113	102	92	83	78	72	67	61	55	50
770	780	126	116	105	95	85	79	74	68	62	57	51
780	790	129	119	108	98	87	81	75	70	64	58	53
790	800	132	121	111	100	90	82	77	71	65	60	54
800	810	135	124	114	103	93	84	78	73	67	61	56
810	820	137	127	116	106	95	85	80	74	68	63	57
820	830	140	130	119	109	98	88	81	76	70	64	59
830	840	143	133	122	112	101	91	83	77	71	66	60
840	850	146	135	125	114	104	93	84	79	73	67	62
850	860	149	138	128	117	107	96	86	80	74	69	63
860	870	151	141	130	120	109	99	88	82	76	70	65
870	880	154	144	133	123	112	102	91	83	77	72	66
880	890	157	147	136	126	115	105	94	85	79	73	68
890	900	160	149	139	128	118	107	97	86	80	75	69
900	910	163	152	142	131	121	110	100	89	82	76	71
910	920	165	155	144	134	123	113	102	92	83	78	72
920	930	168	158	147	137	126	116	105	95	85	79	74
930	940	171	161	150	140	129	119	108	98	87	81	75
940	950	174	163	153	142	132	121	111	100	90	82	77
950	960	177	166	156	145	135	124	114	103	93	84	78
At least	But less than	0	1	2	3	4	5	6	7	8	9	10 or more
960	970	179	169	158	148	137	127	116	106	95	85	80
970	980	182	172	161	151	140	130	119	109	98	88	81
980	990	185	175	164	154	143	133	122	112	101	91	83
990	1,000	188	177	167	156	146	135	125	114	104	93	84
1,000	1,010	191	180	170	159	149	138	128	117	107	96	86
1,010	1,020	193	183	172	162	151	141	130	120	109	99	88
1,020	1,030	196	186	175	165	154	144	133	123	112	102	91
1,030	1,040	199	189	178	168	157	147	136	126	115	105	94
1,040	1,050	202	191	181	170	160	149	139	128	118	107	97
1,050	1,060	205	194	184	173	163	152	142	131	121	110	100
1,060	1,070	207	197	186	176	165	155	144	134	123	113	102
1,070	1,080	210	200	189	179	168	158	147	137	126	116	105
1,080	1,090	213	203	192	182	171	161	150	140	129	119	108
1,090	1,100	216	205	195	184	174	163	153	142	132	121	111
1,100	1,110	219	208	198	187	177	166	156	145	135	124	114
1,110	1,120	221	211	200	190	179	169	158	148	137	127	116
1,120	1,130	224	214	203	193	182	172	161	151	140	130	119
1,130	1,140	227	217	206	196	185	175	164	154	143	133	122
1,140	1,150	230	219	209	198	188	177	167	156	146	135	125
1,150	1,160	233	222	212	201	191	180	170	159	149	138	128
1,160	1,170	235	225	214	204	193	183	172	162	151	141	130
1,170	1,180	238	228	217	207	196	186	175	165	154	144	133
1,180	1,190	241	231	220	210	199	189	178	168	157	147	136
1,190	1,200	244	233	223	212	202	191	181	170	160	149	139
1,200	1,210	247	236	226	215	205	194	184	173	163	152	142
1,210	1,220	249	239	228	218	207	197	186	176	165	155	144
1,220	1,230	252	242	231	221	210	200	189	179	168	158	147
1,230	1,240	255	245	234	224	213	203	192	182	171	161	150
1,240	1,250	258	247	237	226	216	205	195	184	174	163	153
1,250	1,260	261	250	240	229	219	208	198	187	177	166	156
1,260	1,270	263	253	242	232	221	211	200	190	179	169	158

Name ______________________________

Exercise 10A1 or 10B1

1.

2.

JOURNAL PAGE

	DATE		DESCRIPTION	POST. REF.	DEBIT	CREDIT	
1							1
2							2
3							3
4							4
5							5
6							6
7							7

Exercise 10A2 or 10B2

JOURNAL PAGE

	DATE		DESCRIPTION	POST. REF.	DEBIT	CREDIT	
1							1
2							2
3							3
4							4
5							5

Exercise 10A3 or 10B3

Name	Taxable Earnings FICA	Unemploy.
Adams/Carlson		
Ellis/Davis		
Lewis		
Mason/Nixon		
Yates/Shippe		
Zielke/Watts		
Total		

JOURNAL PAGE

	DATE		DESCRIPTION	POST. REF.	DEBIT	CREDIT	
1							1
2							2
3							3
4							4

Exercise 10A4 or 10B4

JOURNAL PAGE

	DATE		DESCRIPTION	POST. REF.	DEBIT	CREDIT	
1							1
2							2
3							3
4							4
5							5
6							6
7							7
8							8
9							9
10							10

Exercise 10A5 or 10B5

Exercise 10A6 or 10B6

1.

JOURNAL PAGE

	DATE		DESCRIPTION	POST. REF.	DEBIT	CREDIT	
1							1
2							2
3							3
4							4
5							5

2.

JOURNAL PAGE

	DATE		DESCRIPTION	POST. REF.	DEBIT	CREDIT	
1							1
2							2
3							3
4							4
5							5

Problem 10A1 or 10B1

1.

Name	Taxable Earnings: Unemploy. Comp.	Taxable Earnings: FICA
Barnum/Ackers		
Duel/Conley		
Hunt/Davis		
Larson/Lawrence		
Miller/Rawlings		
Swan/Tester		
Yates/Wray		
Total		

2.

JOURNAL PAGE

	DATE	DESCRIPTION	POST. REF.	DEBIT	CREDIT	
1						1
2						2
3						3
4						4
5						5
6						6
7						7
8						8
9						9
10						10
11						11

Problem 10A2 or 10B2

1.

JOURNAL

PAGE

DATE		DESCRIPTION	POST. REF.	DEBIT	CREDIT
July	15	FICA Tax payable	211	1800 00	
		Employee income Tax pay	214	1015 00	
		Cash	111		2815 00
		To record 941 deposit			
		for FICA and federal			
		income Tax withheld			
	31	Wages & salary expense	542	12000 00	
		Employee income Tax pay	214		1020 00
		saving Bonds payable	211		900 00
		Cash	261		350 00
		To record July payroll	111		9730 00
	31	Saving Bonds payable	261	700 00	
		Cash	111		700 00
		Purchase of U.S. saving			
		Bonds for employees.			
	31	Payroll Taxes Expense	552	1086 00	
		FICA Tax payable	211		900 00
		FUTA Tax payable	212		24 00
		SUTA Tax Payable	213		162 00
		Employers payroll			
		taxes for month of July			
Aug	15	FICA Tax payable	211	1800 00	
		Employee income Tax	214	1020 00	
		cash	111		2820 00
		941 Deposit			
	15	SUTA Tax payable	213	972 00	
		Cash	111		972 00

Problem 10A2 or 10B2 (Continued)

JOURNAL

PAGE

DATE		DESCRIPTION	POST. REF.	DEBIT	CREDIT
Aug	15	FUTA Tax Payable	212	188 00	
		Cash			188 00
		Paid federal unemployment			
		Tax			

Problem 10A2 or 10B2 (Concluded)

2.

Cash 111

Debit	Credit
56,200	2,815
	9,730
	700
	2,820
	972
	186

FICA Tax Payable 211

Debit	Credit
1,800	1,800
	900
	900
1,800	

FUTA Tax Payable 212

Debit	Credit
	164
188	24

SUTA Tax Payable 213

Debit	Credit
	810
	162
972	

Employ. Inc. Tax Pay. 214

Debit	Credit
1,015	1,015
1,020	1,020

Savings Bonds Payable 261

Debit	Credit
	350
	350
700	

Wages and Salary Expense 542

Debit	Credit
12,000	

Payroll Taxes Expense 552

Debit	Credit
1,086	

Problem 10A3 or 10B3

1. 650,000 x .003 = $1,950.00

JOURNAL PAGE

	DATE		DESCRIPTION	POST. REF.	DEBIT	CREDIT	
1	Jan 19--	2	Worker's comp Ins exp.		1950 00		1
2			Cash			1950 00	2
3			Paid insurance premium				3
4							4
5							5
6							6

2.
672,000 x .003 = 2,016.00
Less estimate = 1,950.00
Additional due = 66.00

JOURNAL PAGE

	DATE		DESCRIPTION	POST. REF.	DEBIT	CREDIT	
1	Dec	31	Workers Compensation Insurance		66 00		1
2			Exp). Workers Compensation			66 00	2
3			Insurance payable				3
4			Adjustment for Ins. premium				4
5							5
6							6

Name ____________________

Problem 10A3 or 10B3 (Concluded)

3.

$634,000 x .003 = $1,902.00
Less estimate pr. paid 1,950.00
refund due. 48.00

JOURNAL PAGE

	DATE		DESCRIPTION	POST. REF.	DEBIT	CREDIT	
1	Dec	31	Insurance Refund Receivable		48 00		1
2			Workers Compensation exp.			48 00	2
3			Adj for Ins. premium				3
4							4
5							5
6							6
7							7
8							8
9							9
10							10
11							11
12							12
13							13
14							14
15							15
16							16
17							17
18							18
19							19
20							20
21							21

Mastery Problem

JOURNAL PAGE

	DATE		DESCRIPTION	POST. REF.	DEBIT	CREDIT	
1							1
2							2
3							3
4							4
5							5
6							6
7							7
8							8
9							9
10							10
11							11
12							12
13							13
14							14
15							15
16							16
17							17
18							18
19							19
20							20
21							21
22							22
23							23
24							24
25							25
26							26
27							27
28							28
29							29
30							30
31							31
32							32
33							33

Mastery Problem (Concluded)

JOURNAL PAGE

	DATE		DESCRIPTION	POST. REF.	DEBIT	CREDIT	
1							1
2							2
3							3
4							4
5							5
6							6
7							7
8							8
9							9
10							10
11							11
12							12
13							13
14							14
15							15
16							16
17							17
18							18
19							19
20							20
21							21
22							22
23							23
24							24
25							25
26							26
27							27
28							28
29							29
30							30
31							31
32							32
33							33

Name ______________________________

Exercise 11A1 or 11B1

1. ____________________ 5. ____________________
2. ____________________ 6. ____________________
3. ____________________ 7. ____________________
4. ____________________

Exercise 11A2 or 11B2

1.

Cash

Accounts Receivable

Sales

2.

Cash

Accounts Receivable

Sales Tax Payable

Sales

3.

Cash

Accounts Receivable

Sales Returns & Allowances

Sales

Exercise 11A2 or 11B2 (Concluded)

4.

Cash

Accounts Receivable

Sales Tax Payable

Sales Return & Allowances

Sales

5.

Cash

Accounts Receivable

Sales

Sales Discounts

Exercise 11A3 or 11B3

Name ____

Exercise 11A4 or 11B4

a.

JOURNAL PAGE

	DATE		DESCRIPTION	POST. REF.	DEBIT	CREDIT	
1							1
2							2
3							3
4							4
5							5
6							6
7							7
8							8
9							9
10							10
11							11
12							12
13							13
14							14
15							15
16							16
17							17
18							18
19							19
20							20

b.

SALES JOURNAL PAGE

DATE		SALE NO.	TO WHOM SOLD	POST REF.	ACCOUNTS RECEIVABLE DR.	SALES CR.	SALES TAX PAYABLE CR.

Exercise 11A5 or 11B5

JOURNAL

PAGE *60*

	DATE		DESCRIPTION	POST. REF.	DEBIT	CREDIT	
1							1
2							2
3							3
4							4
5							5
6							6
7							7
8							8
9							9
10							10
11							11
12							12
13							13
14							14
15							15

GENERAL LEDGER

ACCOUNT ACCOUNT NO.

DATE		ITEM	POST. REF.	DEBIT	CREDIT	BALANCE	
						DEBIT	CREDIT

ACCOUNT ACCOUNT NO.

DATE		ITEM	POST. REF.	DEBIT	CREDIT	BALANCE	
						DEBIT	CREDIT

Name ______________________

Exercise 11A5 or 11B5 (Concluded)

ACCOUNTS RECEIVABLE LEDGER

NAME *John B. Adams* TERMS

ADDRESS *3201 West Judkins Road, Seattle, WA 98201*

DATE		ITEM	POST. REF.	DEBIT	CREDIT	BALANCE
19-- June	1	Balance	✓			850 00

NAME *Marie L. Philips* TERMS

ADDRESS *158 West Adams Point, Bellvue, WA 98401*

DATE		ITEM	POST. REF.	DEBIT	CREDIT	BALANCE
19-- June	1	Balance	✓			1,018 00

NAME *L. B. Greene* TERMS

ADDRESS *44 Western Blvd., Spokane, WA 98601*

DATE		ITEM	POST. REF.	DEBIT	CREDIT	BALANCE
19-- June	1	Balance	✓			428 00

Exercise 11A6 or 11B6

a.

JOURNAL

PAGE

	DATE		DESCRIPTION	POST. REF.	DEBIT	CREDIT	
1							1
2							2
3							3
4							4
5							5
6							6
7							7
8							8
9							9
10							10
11							11
12							12
13							13
14							14
15							15
16							16

b.

CASH RECEIPTS JOURNAL

PAGE

	DATE		ACCOUNT CREDITED	POST REF.	GENERAL CR.	ACCOUNTS RECEIV. CR.	SALES CR.	SALES TAX PAY. CR.	CASH DR.	
1										1
2										2
3										3
4										4
5										5
6										6
7										7
8										8
9										9
10										10
11										11

Name ______________________________

Exercise 11A7 or 11B7

Problem 11A1 or 11B1

1.

SALES JOURNAL PAGE 8

DATE	SALE NO.	TO WHOM SOLD	POST REF.	ACCOUNTS RECEIVABLE DR.	SALES CR.	SALES TAX PAYABLE CR.

GENERAL LEDGER

2.

ACCOUNT *Accounts Receivable* ACCOUNT NO. *111*

DATE	ITEM	POST. REF.	DEBIT	CREDIT	BALANCE DEBIT	BALANCE CREDIT

ACCOUNT *Sales Tax Payable* ACCOUNT NO. *212*

DATE	ITEM	POST. REF.	DEBIT	CREDIT	BALANCE DEBIT	BALANCE CREDIT

Name ______________________

Problem 11A1 or 11B1 (Concluded)

ACCOUNT *Sales* ACCOUNT NO. *411*

DATE		ITEM	POST. REF.	DEBIT	CREDIT	BALANCE DEBIT	BALANCE CREDIT

ACCOUNTS RECEIVABLE LEDGER

NAME *Jones Manufacturing Co.* TERMS

ADDRESS *8825 Old State Road, Bloomington, IN 47401-8823*

DATE		ITEM	POST. REF.	DEBIT	CREDIT	BALANCE

NAME *Andy Harris, Inc.* TERMS

ADDRESS *125 Fishers Drive, Noblesville, IN 47870-8867*

DATE		ITEM	POST. REF.	DEBIT	CREDIT	BALANCE

NAME *Ardis Mckenzie* TERMS

ADDRESS *2100 Greer Lane, Bedford, IN 47421-8876*

DATE		ITEM	POST. REF.	DEBIT	CREDIT	BALANCE

NAME *R. B. Smith & Co.* TERMS

ADDRESS *1225 W. Temperance Street, Elletsville, IN 47429-9976*

DATE		ITEM	POST. REF.	DEBIT	CREDIT	BALANCE

Problem 11A2 or 11B2

1.

CASH RECEIPTS JOURNAL

PAGE *10*

	DATE		ACCOUNT CREDITED	POST REF.	GENERAL CR.	ACCOUNTS RECEIV. CR.	SALES CR.	SALES TAX PAY. CR.	BANK CREDIT CARD EXP. DR.	CASH DR.	
1											1
2											2
3											3
4											4
5											5
6											6
7											7
8											8
9											9
10											10
11											11
12											12
13											13
14											14

Name ______________________________

Problem 11A2 or 11B2 (Continued)

JOURNAL PAGE *8*

	DATE	DESCRIPTION	POST. REF.	DEBIT	CREDIT	
1						1
2						2
3						3
4						4
5						5
6						6
7						7
8						8
9						9
10						10
11						11
12						12
13						13
14						14

Problem 11A2 only

2.

GENERAL LEDGER

ACCOUNT *Cash* ACCOUNT NO. *101*

DATE		ITEM	POST. REF.	DEBIT	CREDIT	BALANCE DEBIT	BALANCE CREDIT
19-- *Dec.*	*1*	*Balance*	✓			*9,862.00*	

ACCOUNT *Accounts Receivable* ACCOUNT NO. *111*

DATE		ITEM	POST. REF.	DEBIT	CREDIT	BALANCE DEBIT	BALANCE CREDIT
19-- *Dec.*	*1*	*Balance*	✓			*9,352.00*	

Problem 11A2 (Continued)

ACCOUNT *Sales Tax Payable* ACCOUNT NO. *212*

DATE	ITEM	POST. REF.	DEBIT	CREDIT	BALANCE DEBIT	BALANCE CREDIT

ACCOUNT *Sales* ACCOUNT NO. *411*

DATE	ITEM	POST. REF.	DEBIT	CREDIT	BALANCE DEBIT	BALANCE CREDIT

ACCOUNT *Sales Returns & Allowances* ACCOUNT NO. *412*

DATE	ITEM	POST. REF.	DEBIT	CREDIT	BALANCE DEBIT	BALANCE CREDIT

ACCOUNT *Bank Credit Card Expense* ACCOUNT NO. *525*

DATE	ITEM	POST. REF.	DEBIT	CREDIT	BALANCE DEBIT	BALANCE CREDIT

ACCOUNTS RECEIVABLE LEDGER

NAME *Michael Anderson* TERMS

ADDRESS *233 West 11th Avenue, Detroit, MI 59500*

DATE		ITEM	POST. REF.	DEBIT	CREDIT	BALANCE
19-- *Dec.*	*1*	*Balance*	✓			*2 4 8 0 00*

Problem 11A2 (Concluded)

NAME *Ansel Manufacturing* TERMS

ADDRESS *284 West 58 Street, Detroit, MI 59522*

DATE		ITEM	POST. REF.	DEBIT	CREDIT	BALANCE
19-- Dec.	1	Balance	✓			982 00

NAME *W. J. Beemer* TERMS

ADDRESS *P.O. Box 864, Detroit, MI 59552*

DATE		ITEM	POST. REF.	DEBIT	CREDIT	BALANCE
19-- Dec.	1	Balance	✓			880 00

NAME *Rachel Carson* TERMS

ADDRESS *11312 Fourteenth Avenue South, Detroit, MI 59221*

DATE		ITEM	POST. REF.	DEBIT	CREDIT	BALANCE
19-- Dec.	1	Balance	✓			3200 00

NAME *Tom Wilson* TERMS

ADDRESS *100 NW Seward St., Detroit, MI 59210*

DATE		ITEM	POST. REF.	DEBIT	CREDIT	BALANCE
19-- Dec.	1	Balance	✓			1810 00

Problem 11B2 only (Continued)

2.

GENERAL LEDGER

ACCOUNT *Cash* ACCOUNT NO. *101*

DATE		ITEM	POST. REF.	DEBIT	CREDIT	BALANCE DEBIT	BALANCE CREDIT
19-- Jan.	1	Balance	✓			2,890.75	

ACCOUNT *Accounts Receivable* ACCOUNT NO. *111*

DATE		ITEM	POST. REF.	DEBIT	CREDIT	BALANCE DEBIT	BALANCE CREDIT
19-- Jan.	1	Balance	✓			6,300.00	

ACCOUNT *Sales Tax Payable* ACCOUNT NO. *212*

DATE		ITEM	POST. REF.	DEBIT	CREDIT	BALANCE DEBIT	BALANCE CREDIT

ACCOUNT *Sales* ACCOUNT NO. *411*

DATE		ITEM	POST. REF.	DEBIT	CREDIT	BALANCE DEBIT	BALANCE CREDIT

Problem 11B2 (Continued)

ACCOUNT *Sales Returns & Allowances* ACCOUNT NO. *412*

DATE		ITEM	POST. REF.	DEBIT	CREDIT	BALANCE DEBIT	BALANCE CREDIT

ACCOUNT *Bank Credit Card Expense* ACCOUNT NO. *525*

DATE		ITEM	POST. REF.	DEBIT	CREDIT	BALANCE DEBIT	BALANCE CREDIT

ACCOUNTS RECEIVABLE LEDGER

NAME *Michael Anderson* TERMS

ADDRESS *233 West 11th Avenue, Detroit, MI 59500*

DATE		ITEM	POST. REF.	DEBIT	CREDIT	BALANCE
19-- *Jan.*	*1*	*Balance*	✓			*1 4 0 0 00*

NAME *Ansel Manufacturing* TERMS

ADDRESS *284 West 88 Street, Detroit, MI 59522*

DATE		ITEM	POST. REF.	DEBIT	CREDIT	BALANCE
19-- *Jan.*	*1*	*Balance*	✓			*3 1 8 00*

Problem 11B2 (Concluded)

NAME *W. J. Beemer* TERMS

ADDRESS *P.O. Box 564, Detroit, MI 59552*

DATE		ITEM	POST. REF.	DEBIT	CREDIT	BALANCE
19-- Jan.	1	Balance	✓			815 00

NAME *Rachel Carson* TERMS

ADDRESS *11312 Fourteenth Avenue South, Detroit, MI 59221*

DATE		ITEM	POST. REF.	DEBIT	CREDIT	BALANCE
19-- Jan.	1	Balance	✓			1481 00

NAME *Tom Wilson* TERMS

ADDRESS *100 NW Seward St., Detroit, MI 59210*

DATE		ITEM	POST. REF.	DEBIT	CREDIT	BALANCE
19-- Jan.	1	Balance	✓			2286 00

Name ______________________________

Problem 11A3 or 11B3

1.

SALES JOURNAL

PAGE 6

DATE		SALE NO.	TO WHOM SOLD	POST REF.	ACCOUNTS RECEIVABLE DR.	SALES CR.	SALES TAX PAYABLE CR.

CASH RECEIPTS JOURNAL

PAGE 9

DATE		ACCOUNT CREDITED	POST REF.	GENERAL CR.	ACCOUNTS RECEIV. CR.	SALES CR.	SALES TAX PAY. CR.	CASH DR.

Problem 11A3 or 11B3 (Continued)

JOURNAL

PAGE *5*

	DATE		DESCRIPTION	POST. REF.	DEBIT	CREDIT	
1							1
2							2
3							3
4							4
5							5
6							6
7							7
8							8
9							9
10							10
11							11

Problem 11A3 only

2.

GENERAL LEDGER

ACCOUNT *Cash* ACCOUNT NO. *101*

DATE		ITEM	POST. REF.	DEBIT	CREDIT	BALANCE DEBIT	BALANCE CREDIT
19-- *Mar.*	*1*	*Balance*	✓			*9,741.00*	

ACCOUNT *Accounts Receivable* ACCOUNT NO. *111*

DATE		ITEM	POST. REF.	DEBIT	CREDIT	BALANCE DEBIT	BALANCE CREDIT
19-- *Mar.*	*1*	*Balance*	✓			*10,582.5*	

Problem 11A3 (Continued)

ACCOUNT *Sales Tax Payable* ACCOUNT NO. *212*

DATE	ITEM	POST. REF.	DEBIT	CREDIT	BALANCE DEBIT	BALANCE CREDIT

ACCOUNT *Sales* ACCOUNT NO. *411*

DATE	ITEM	POST. REF.	DEBIT	CREDIT	BALANCE DEBIT	BALANCE CREDIT

ACCOUNT *Sales Returns & Allowances* ACCOUNT NO. *412*

DATE	ITEM	POST. REF.	DEBIT	CREDIT	BALANCE DEBIT	BALANCE CREDIT

ACCOUNTS RECEIVABLE LEDGER

NAME *Able & Co.* TERMS

ADDRESS *1424 Jackson Creek Road, Nashville, IN 47448-2245*

DATE	ITEM	POST. REF.	DEBIT	CREDIT	BALANCE

Problem 11A3 (Concluded)

NAME *Blevins Bakery* TERMS

ADDRESS *6422 E. Bender Road, Bloomington, IN 47401-7756*

DATE		ITEM	POST. REF.	DEBIT	CREDIT	BALANCE

NAME *R. J. Kalas* TERMS

ADDRESS *3315 Longview Ave., Bloomington, IN 47401-7223*

DATE		ITEM	POST. REF.	DEBIT	CREDIT	BALANCE

NAME *Thompson Group* TERMS

ADDRESS *2300 E. National Road, Cumberland, IN 46229-4824*

DATE		ITEM	POST. REF.	DEBIT	CREDIT	BALANCE
19-- *Mar.*	*1*	*Balance*	✓			*1 0 5 8 25*

Problem 11B3 only

2.

GENERAL LEDGER

ACCOUNT *Cash* ACCOUNT NO. *101*

DATE		ITEM	POST. REF.	DEBIT	CREDIT	BALANCE DEBIT	BALANCE CREDIT
19-- *Apr.*	*1*	*Balance*	✓			*2 8 6 4 54*	

Problem 11B3 (Continued)

ACCOUNT *Accounts Receivable* ACCOUNT NO. *111*

DATE		ITEM	POST. REF.	DEBIT	CREDIT	BALANCE DEBIT	BALANCE CREDIT
19-- Apr.	1	Balance	✓			2,726.25	

ACCOUNT *Sales Tax Payable* ACCOUNT NO. *212*

DATE		ITEM	POST. REF.	DEBIT	CREDIT	BALANCE DEBIT	BALANCE CREDIT

ACCOUNT *Sales* ACCOUNT NO. *411*

DATE		ITEM	POST. REF.	DEBIT	CREDIT	BALANCE DEBIT	BALANCE CREDIT

ACCOUNT *Sales Returns & Allowances* ACCOUNT NO. *412*

DATE		ITEM	POST. REF.	DEBIT	CREDIT	BALANCE DEBIT	BALANCE CREDIT

Problem 11B3 (Concluded)

ACCOUNTS RECEIVABLE LEDGER

NAME *O. L. Meyers* TERMS

ADDRESS *1424 Jackson Creek Road, Nashville, IN 47448-2245*

DATE		ITEM	POST. REF.	DEBIT	CREDIT	BALANCE
19-- Apr.	1	Balance	✓			2 186 00

NAME *Kelsay Munkres* TERMS

ADDRESS *6422 E. Bender Road, Bloomington, IN 47401-7756*

DATE		ITEM	POST. REF.	DEBIT	CREDIT	BALANCE
19-- Apr.	1	Balance	✓			482 00

NAME *Andrew Plaa* TERMS

ADDRESS *3315 Longview Ave., Bloomington, IN 47401-7223*

DATE		ITEM	POST. REF.	DEBIT	CREDIT	BALANCE

NAME *Melissa Richfield* TERMS

ADDRESS *2300 E. National Road, Cumberland, IN 46229-4824*

DATE		ITEM	POST. REF.	DEBIT	CREDIT	BALANCE
19-- Apr.	1	Balance	✓			58 25

Problem 11A4 or 11B4

Mastery Problem

1. and 2.

SALES JOURNAL PAGE 3

DATE		SALE NO.	TO WHOM SOLD	POST REF.	ACCOUNTS RECEIVABLE DR.	SALES CR.	SALES TAX PAYABLE CR.

Mastery Problem (Continued)

CASH RECEIPTS JOURNAL PAGE 21

DATE		ACCOUNT CREDITED	POST REF.	GENERAL CR.	ACCOUNTS RECEIV. CR.	SALES CR.	SALES TAX PAY. CR.	CASH DR.

Mastery Problem (Continued)

JOURNAL PAGE 7

	DATE		DESCRIPTION	POST. REF.	DEBIT	CREDIT	
1							1
2							2
3							3
4							4
5							5
6							6
7							7
8							8

3.

GENERAL LEDGER

ACCOUNT *Cash* ACCOUNT NO. *111*

DATE		ITEM	POST. REF.	DEBIT	CREDIT	BALANCE DEBIT	BALANCE CREDIT
19-- *Sept.*	*1*	*Balance*	✓			*23 5 0 0 25*	

ACCOUNT *Accounts Receivable* ACCOUNT NO. *131*

DATE		ITEM	POST. REF.	DEBIT	CREDIT	BALANCE DEBIT	BALANCE CREDIT
19-- *Sept.*	*1*	*Balance*	✓			*8 5 0 75*	

ACCOUNT *Notes Payable* ACCOUNT NO. *216*

DATE		ITEM	POST. REF.	DEBIT	CREDIT	BALANCE DEBIT	BALANCE CREDIT
19-- *Sept.*	*1*	*Balance*	✓				*2 5 0 0 00*

Mastery Problem (Continued)

ACCOUNT *Sales Tax Payable* ACCOUNT NO. *221*

DATE		ITEM	POST. REF.	DEBIT	CREDIT	BALANCE DEBIT	BALANCE CREDIT
19-- *Sept.*	*1*	*Balance*	✓				*1 1 5 00*

ACCOUNT *Sales* ACCOUNT NO. *411*

DATE		ITEM	POST. REF.	DEBIT	CREDIT	BALANCE DEBIT	BALANCE CREDIT

ACCOUNT *Sales Returns & Allowances* ACCOUNT NO. *411.1*

DATE		ITEM	POST. REF.	DEBIT	CREDIT	BALANCE DEBIT	BALANCE CREDIT

ACCOUNT *Boarding and Grooming Revenue* ACCOUNT NO. *412*

DATE		ITEM	POST. REF.	DEBIT	CREDIT	BALANCE DEBIT	BALANCE CREDIT

Mastery Problem (Continued)

ACCOUNTS RECEIVABLE LEDGER

NAME *All American Day Camp* TERMS

ADDRESS *8825 Old State Road, Bloomington, IN 47401-8823*

DATE		ITEM	POST. REF.	DEBIT	CREDIT	BALANCE

NAME *Jayne Brown* TERMS

ADDRESS *125 Fishers Drive, Noblesville, IN 47870-8867*

DATE		ITEM	POST. REF.	DEBIT	CREDIT	BALANCE
19-- *Sept.*	*1*	*Balance*	✓			*456 00*

NAME *Ed Cochran* TERMS

ADDRESS *2100 Greer Lane, Bedford, IN 47421-8876*

DATE		ITEM	POST. REF.	DEBIT	CREDIT	BALANCE
19-- *Sept.*	*1*	*Balance*	✓			*63 25*

NAME *Joe Gloy* TERMS

ADDRESS *1225 W. Temperence Street, Elletsville, IN 47429-9976*

DATE		ITEM	POST. REF.	DEBIT	CREDIT	BALANCE
19-- *Sept.*	*1*	*Balance*	✓			*273 25*

Mastery Problem (Continued)

NAME *Susan Hays* TERMS

ADDRESS *1424 Jackson Creek Road, Nashville, IN 47448-2245*

DATE		ITEM	POST. REF.	DEBIT	CREDIT	BALANCE

NAME *Ken Shank* TERMS

ADDRESS *6422 E. Bender Road, Bloomington, IN 47401-7756*

DATE		ITEM	POST. REF.	DEBIT	CREDIT	BALANCE

NAME *Tully Shaw* TERMS

ADDRESS *3315 Longview Ave., Bloomington, IN 47401-7223*

DATE		ITEM	POST. REF.	DEBIT	CREDIT	BALANCE

NAME *Nancy Truelove* TERMS

ADDRESS *2300 E. National Road, Cumberland, IN 46229-4824*

DATE		ITEM	POST. REF.	DEBIT	CREDIT	BALANCE
19-- *Sept.*	*1*	*Balance*	✓			*58 25*

Mastery Problem (Concluded)

NAME *Jean Warkentin* TERMS

ADDRESS *1813 Deep Well Court, Bloomington, IN 47401-5124*

DATE		ITEM	POST. REF.	DEBIT	CREDIT	BALANCE

4.

5.

Exercise 12A1 or 12B1

1. ______________________
2. ______________________
3. ______________________
4. ______________________

Exercise 12A2 or 12B2

1.

2.

3.

JOURNAL PAGE

	DATE		DESCRIPTION	POST. REF.	DEBIT	CREDIT	
1							1
2							2
3							3
4							4
5							5
6							6
7							7
8							8
9							9
10							10
11							11
12							12

Exercise 12A3 or 12B3

1.

Cash

Accounts Payable

Purchases

Purchases Returns & Allow.

Purchases Discounts

Freight-In

2.

Cash

Accounts Payable

Purchases

Purchases Returns & Allow.

Purchases Discounts

Freight-In

Exercise 12A3 or 12B3 (Concluded)

3.

Cash

Accounts Payable

Purchases

Purchases Returns & Allow.

Purchases Discounts

Freight-In

4.

Cash

Accounts Payable

Purchases

Purchases Returns & Allow.

Purchases Discounts

Freight-In

Exercise 12A4 or 12B4

Name ____________________

Exercise 12A5 or 12B5

1.

JOURNAL

PAGE

	DATE		DESCRIPTION	POST. REF.	DEBIT	CREDIT	
1							1
2							2
3							3
4							4
5							5
6							6
7							7
8							8
9							9
10							10
11							11
12							12
13							13
14							14
15							15
16							16

2.

PURCHASES JOURNAL

PAGE

	DATE		INVOICE NO.	FROM WHOM PURCHASED	POST REF.	PURCHASES DR. ACCTS. PAY. CR.	
1							1
2							2
3							3
4							4
5							5
6							6
7							7
8							8
9							9
10							10
11							11

Exercise 12A6 or 12B6

JOURNAL

PAGE *3*

	DATE		DESCRIPTION	POST. REF.	DEBIT	CREDIT	
1							1
2							2
3							3
4							4
5							5
6							6
7							7
8							8
9							9
10							10
11							11
12							12
13							13

GENERAL LEDGER

ACCOUNT *Accounts Payable* ACCOUNT NO. *218*

DATE		ITEM	POST. REF.	DEBIT	CREDIT	BALANCE	
						DEBIT	CREDIT

ACCOUNT *Purchases Returns and Allowances* ACCOUNT NO. *511.1*

DATE		ITEM	POST. REF.	DEBIT	CREDIT	BALANCE	
						DEBIT	CREDIT

Name ______________________________

Exercise 12A6 or 12B6 (Concluded)

ACCOUNTS PAYABLE LEDGER

NAME ______________________________ TERMS ______

ADDRESS ______________________________

DATE		ITEM	POST. REF.	DEBIT	CREDIT	BALANCE

NAME ______________________________ TERMS ______

ADDRESS ______________________________

DATE		ITEM	POST. REF.	DEBIT	CREDIT	BALANCE

NAME ______________________________ TERMS ______

ADDRESS ______________________________

DATE		ITEM	POST. REF.	DEBIT	CREDIT	BALANCE

Exercise 12A7 or 12B7

CASH PAYMENTS JOURNAL

PAGE

DATE	CK. NO.	ACCOUNT DEBITED	POST REF.	GENERAL DR.	ACCOUNTS PAYABLE DR.	PURCHASES DR.	PURCHASES DISCOUNT CR.	CASH CR.

Name ______________________________

Exercise 12A8 or 12B8

Problem 12A1 or 12B1

1.

PURCHASES JOURNAL — PAGE 7

	DATE		INVOICE NO.	FROM WHOM PURCHASED	POST REF.	PURCHASES DR. ACCTS. PAY. CR.	
1							1
2							2
3							3
4							4
5							5
6							6
7							7
8							8
9							9

2.

GENERAL LEDGER

ACCOUNT *Accounts Payable* — ACCOUNT NO. *218*

DATE		ITEM	POST. REF.	DEBIT	CREDIT	BALANCE	
						DEBIT	CREDIT

ACCOUNT *Purchases* — ACCOUNT NO. *511*

DATE		ITEM	POST. REF.	DEBIT	CREDIT	BALANCE	
						DEBIT	CREDIT

ACCOUNTS PAYABLE LEDGER

NAME — TERMS

ADDRESS

DATE		ITEM	POST. REF.	DEBIT	CREDIT	BALANCE

Problem 12A1 or 12B1 (Concluded)

NAME TERMS

ADDRESS

DATE		ITEM	POST. REF.	DEBIT	CREDIT	BALANCE

NAME TERMS

ADDRESS

DATE		ITEM	POST. REF.	DEBIT	CREDIT	BALANCE

NAME TERMS

ADDRESS

DATE		ITEM	POST. REF.	DEBIT	CREDIT	BALANCE

NAME TERMS

ADDRESS

DATE		ITEM	POST. REF.	DEBIT	CREDIT	BALANCE

Problem 12A2 or 12B2

1.

GENERAL LEDGER

ACCOUNT *Accounts Payable* ACCOUNT NO. *218*

DATE		ITEM	POST. REF.	DEBIT	CREDIT	BALANCE	
						DEBIT	CREDIT

ACCOUNT *Purchases* ACCOUNT NO. *511*

DATE		ITEM	POST. REF.	DEBIT	CREDIT	BALANCE	
						DEBIT	CREDIT

ACCOUNTS PAYABLE LEDGER

NAME TERMS

ADDRESS

DATE		ITEM	POST. REF.	DEBIT	CREDIT	BALANCE

NAME TERMS

ADDRESS

DATE		ITEM	POST. REF.	DEBIT	CREDIT	BALANCE

Name ______________________________

Problem 12A2 or 12B2 (Concluded)

ACCOUNTS PAYABLE LEDGER

NAME ______________________ TERMS ______

ADDRESS ______________________

DATE		ITEM	POST. REF.	DEBIT	CREDIT	BALANCE

NAME ______________________ TERMS ______

ADDRESS ______________________

DATE		ITEM	POST. REF.	DEBIT	CREDIT	BALANCE

NAME ______________________ TERMS ______

ADDRESS ______________________

DATE		ITEM	POST. REF.	DEBIT	CREDIT	BALANCE

Problem 12A3 or 12B3

1.

CASH PAYMENTS JOURNAL

PAGE 6

DATE		CK. NO.	ACCOUNT DEBITED	POST REF.	GENERAL DR.	ACCOUNTS PAYABLE DR.	PURCHASES DR.	PURCHASES DISCOUNT CR.	CASH CR.

Problem 12A3 or 12B3 (Continued)

2.

GENERAL LEDGER

ACCOUNT *Cash* ACCOUNT NO. *111*

DATE		ITEM	POST. REF.	DEBIT	CREDIT	BALANCE DEBIT	BALANCE CREDIT
19-- *May*	*1*	*Balance*	✓			*20 0 0 0 00*	

ACCOUNT *Accounts Payable* ACCOUNT NO. *218*

DATE		ITEM	POST. REF.	DEBIT	CREDIT	BALANCE DEBIT	BALANCE CREDIT
19-- *May*	*1*	*Balance*	✓				*10 0 0 0 00*

ACCOUNT *Purchases* ACCOUNT NO. *511*

DATE		ITEM	POST. REF.	DEBIT	CREDIT	BALANCE DEBIT	BALANCE CREDIT

ACCOUNT *Purchases Discounts* ACCOUNT NO. *511.2*

DATE		ITEM	POST. REF.	DEBIT	CREDIT	BALANCE DEBIT	BALANCE CREDIT

Problem 12A3 or 12B3 (Continued)

ACCOUNT *Freight-In* ACCOUNT NO. *512*

DATE	ITEM	POST. REF.	DEBIT	CREDIT	BALANCE DEBIT	BALANCE CREDIT

ACCOUNT *Rent Expense* ACCOUNT NO. *541*

DATE	ITEM	POST. REF.	DEBIT	CREDIT	BALANCE DEBIT	BALANCE CREDIT

ACCOUNT *Utilities Expense* ACCOUNT NO. *549*

DATE	ITEM	POST. REF.	DEBIT	CREDIT	BALANCE DEBIT	BALANCE CREDIT

ACCOUNTS PAYABLE LEDGER

NAME TERMS

ADDRESS

DATE	ITEM	POST. REF.	DEBIT	CREDIT	BALANCE

Name ______________________________

Problem 12A3 or 12B3 (Concluded)

NAME ______________________________ TERMS ______________

ADDRESS ______________________________

DATE		ITEM	POST. REF.	DEBIT	CREDIT	BALANCE

NAME ______________________________ TERMS ______________

ADDRESS ______________________________

DATE		ITEM	POST. REF.	DEBIT	CREDIT	BALANCE

NAME ______________________________ TERMS ______________

ADDRESS ______________________________

DATE		ITEM	POST. REF.	DEBIT	CREDIT	BALANCE

Problem 12A4 or 12B4

PURCHASES JOURNAL

PAGE 7

	DATE		INVOICE NO.	FROM WHOM PURCHASED	POST REF.	PURCHASES DR. ACCTS. PAY. CR.	
1							1
2							2
3							3
4							4
5							5
6							6
7							7
8							8
9							9
10							10
11							11
12							12
13							13
14							14
15							15
16							16
17							17
18							18
19							19
20							20
21							21
22							22
23							23
24							24
25							25
26							26
27							27
28							28
29							29
30							30
31							31
32							32

Problem 12A4 or 12B4 (Continued)

CASH PAYMENTS JOURNAL

PAGE 9

DATE		CK. NO.	ACCOUNT DEBITED	POST REF.	GENERAL DR.	ACCOUNTS PAYABLE DR.	PURCHASES DR.	PURCHASES DISCOUNT CR.	CASH CR.

Problem 12A4 or 12B4 (Continued)

JOURNAL

PAGE 3

	DATE		DESCRIPTION	POST. REF.	DEBIT	CREDIT	
1							1
2							2
3							3
4							4
5							5
6							6
7							7
8							8
9							9

2.

GENERAL LEDGER

ACCOUNT *Cash* ACCOUNT NO. *111*

DATE		ITEM	POST. REF.	DEBIT	CREDIT	BALANCE DEBIT	BALANCE CREDIT
19-- *July*	*1*	*Balance*	✓			*20 0 0 0 00*	

ACCOUNT *Accounts Payable* ACCOUNT NO. *218*

DATE		ITEM	POST. REF.	DEBIT	CREDIT	BALANCE DEBIT	BALANCE CREDIT

ACCOUNT *, Capital* ACCOUNT NO. *311*

DATE		ITEM	POST. REF.	DEBIT	CREDIT	BALANCE DEBIT	BALANCE CREDIT
19-- *July*	*1*	*Balance*	✓				*20 0 0 0 00*

Problem 12A4 or 12B4 (Continued)

ACCOUNT , *Drawing* ACCOUNT NO. *312*

DATE	ITEM	POST. REF.	DEBIT	CREDIT	BALANCE DEBIT	BALANCE CREDIT

ACCOUNT *Purchases* ACCOUNT NO. *511*

DATE	ITEM	POST. REF.	DEBIT	CREDIT	BALANCE DEBIT	BALANCE CREDIT

ACCOUNT *Purchases Returns and Allowances* ACCOUNT NO. *511.1*

DATE	ITEM	POST. REF.	DEBIT	CREDIT	BALANCE DEBIT	BALANCE CREDIT

ACCOUNT *Purchases Discounts* ACCOUNT NO. *511.2*

DATE	ITEM	POST. REF.	DEBIT	CREDIT	BALANCE DEBIT	BALANCE CREDIT

ACCOUNT *Rent Expense* ACCOUNT NO. *541*

DATE	ITEM	POST. REF.	DEBIT	CREDIT	BALANCE DEBIT	BALANCE CREDIT

Problem 12A4 or 12B4 (Concluded)

ACCOUNTS PAYABLE LEDGER

NAME TERMS

ADDRESS

DATE		ITEM	POST. REF.	DEBIT	CREDIT	BALANCE

NAME TERMS

ADDRESS

DATE		ITEM	POST. REF.	DEBIT	CREDIT	BALANCE

NAME TERMS

ADDRESS

DATE		ITEM	POST. REF.	DEBIT	CREDIT	BALANCE

NAME TERMS

ADDRESS

DATE		ITEM	POST. REF.	DEBIT	CREDIT	BALANCE

Problem 12A5 or 12B5

Mastery Problem

1. and 2.

JOURNAL PAGE 7

	DATE	DESCRIPTION	POST. REF.	DEBIT	CREDIT	
1						1
2						2
3						3
4						4
5						5
6						6
7						7
8						8
9						9
10						10
11						11
12						12
13						13

PURCHASES JOURNAL PAGE 8

	DATE	INVOICE NO.	FROM WHOM PURCHASED	POST REF.	PURCHASES DR. ACCTS. PAY. CR.	
1						1
2						2
3						3
4						4
5						5
6						6
7						7
8						8
9						9
10						10
11						11
12						12
13						13
14						14
15						15

Mastery Problem (Continued)

CASH PAYMENTS JOURNAL

PAGE 12

DATE	CK. NO.	ACCOUNT DEBITED	POST REF.	GENERAL DR.	ACCOUNTS PAYABLE DR.	PURCHASES DR.	PURCHASES DISCOUNT CR.	CASH CR.

Mastery Problem (Continued)

3.

GENERAL LEDGER

ACCOUNT *Cash* ACCOUNT NO. *111*

DATE		ITEM	POST. REF.	DEBIT	CREDIT	BALANCE DEBIT	BALANCE CREDIT
19-- June	1	Balance	✓			32 200 00	

ACCOUNT *Accounts Payable* ACCOUNT NO. *218*

DATE		ITEM	POST. REF.	DEBIT	CREDIT	BALANCE DEBIT	BALANCE CREDIT
19-- June	1	Balance	✓				2 000 00

ACCOUNT *Michelle French, Drawing* ACCOUNT NO. *312*

DATE		ITEM	POST. REF.	DEBIT	CREDIT	BALANCE DEBIT	BALANCE CREDIT
19-- June	1	Balance	✓			18 000 00	

ACCOUNT *Purchases* ACCOUNT NO. *511*

DATE		ITEM	POST. REF.	DEBIT	CREDIT	BALANCE DEBIT	BALANCE CREDIT
19-- June	1	Balance	✓			66 125 66	

Mastery Problem (Continued)

ACCOUNT *Purchases Returns and Allowances* ACCOUNT NO. *511.1*

DATE		ITEM	POST. REF.	DEBIT	CREDIT	BALANCE DEBIT	BALANCE CREDIT
19-- June	1	Balance	✓				2,315.23

ACCOUNT *Purchases Discounts* ACCOUNT NO. *511.2*

DATE		ITEM	POST. REF.	DEBIT	CREDIT	BALANCE DEBIT	BALANCE CREDIT
19-- June	1	Balance	✓				905.00

ACCOUNT *Freight-In* ACCOUNT NO. *512*

DATE		ITEM	POST. REF.	DEBIT	CREDIT	BALANCE DEBIT	BALANCE CREDIT
19-- June	1	Balance	✓			522.60	

ACCOUNT *Rent Expense* ACCOUNT NO. *541*

DATE		ITEM	POST. REF.	DEBIT	CREDIT	BALANCE DEBIT	BALANCE CREDIT
19-- June	1	Balance	✓			3,125.00	

ACCOUNT *Utilities Expense* ACCOUNT NO. *549*

DATE		ITEM	POST. REF.	DEBIT	CREDIT	BALANCE DEBIT	BALANCE CREDIT
19-- June	1	Balance	✓			1,522.87	

Mastery Problem (Continued)

ACCOUNTS PAYABLE LEDGER

NAME *Broadway Publishing Inc.* TERMS *3/10, n/30*

ADDRESS *2300 Goodman, Cincinnati, OH 45219-2901*

DATE		ITEM	POST. REF.	DEBIT	CREDIT	BALANCE

NAME *Irving Publishing Company* TERMS *2/10, n/30*

ADDRESS *5200 N. Keystone Ave., Indianapolis, IN 46220-1986*

DATE		ITEM	POST. REF.	DEBIT	CREDIT	BALANCE

NAME *North-Eastern Publishing Company* TERMS *2/10, n/30*

ADDRESS *874 Crescent Drive, Flint, MI 48503-7564*

DATE		ITEM	POST. REF.	DEBIT	CREDIT	BALANCE
19-- *June*	*1*	*Balance*	✓			*2 0 0 0 00*

NAME *Riley Publishing Company* TERMS *3/10, n/30*

ADDRESS *5675 Pulaski Road, Chicago, IL 60629-6705*

DATE		ITEM	POST. REF.	DEBIT	CREDIT	BALANCE

Mastery Problem (Concluded)

4.

5.

Exercise 13A1 or 13B1

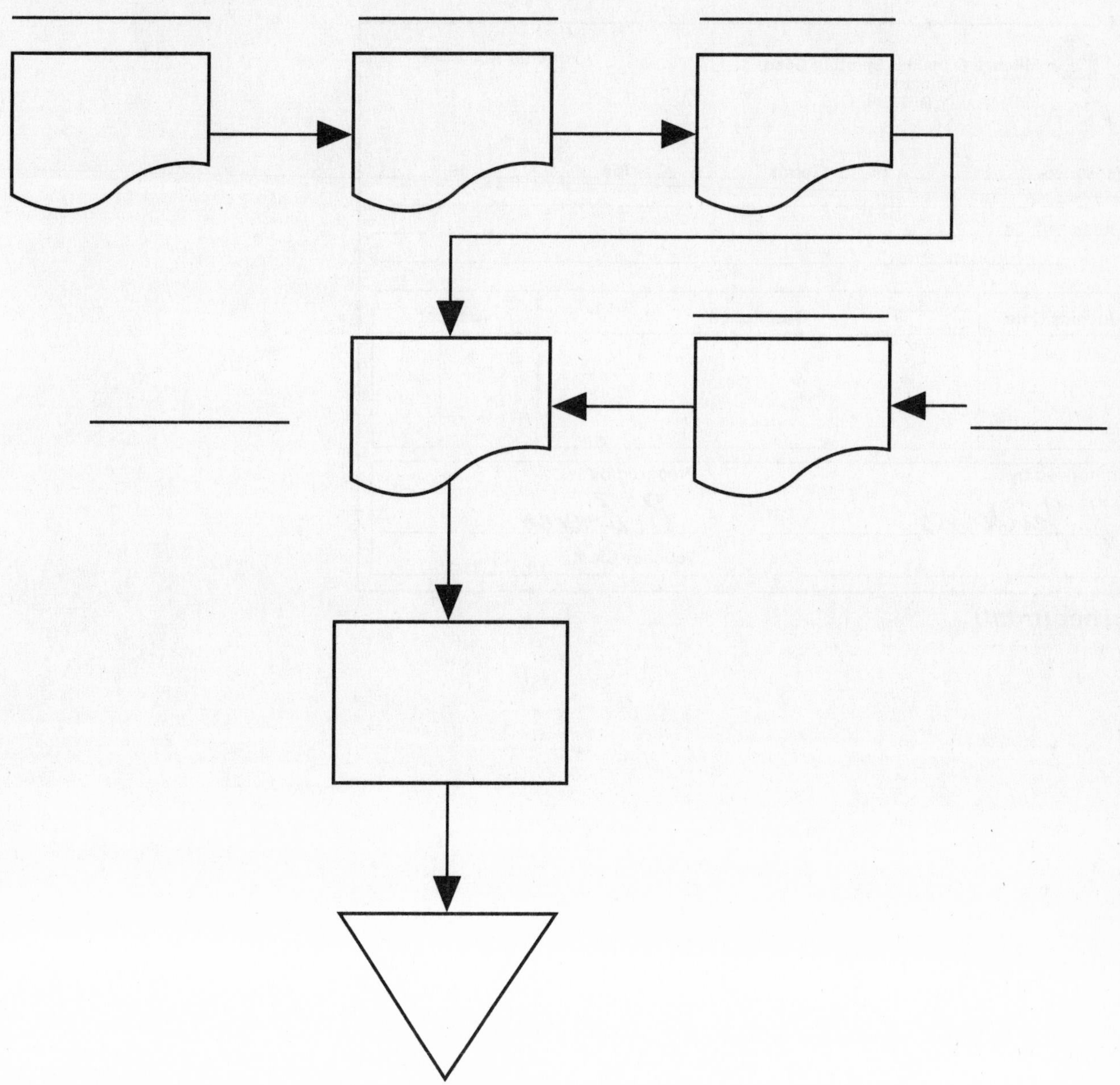

Exercise 13A2 or 13B2

Mitchell & Jenkins Sporting Goods
2200 E. Washington St.
Indianapolis, IN 46201-3216

Voucher No. **164**

Date Issued ____________ 19____ Terms ____________ Due ____________ 19______
To ____
Address ____
____

Invoice Date	Description	Amount	

Authorized by
J. Jenkins

Prepared by
B. Zimmer
Voucher Clerk

Voucher (front)

Account Debited	Acct. No.	Amount

Voucher No. 164
Summary
Invoice ________
Discount ________
Net ________

PAYMENT

Date: ________ Check No. ______ Amount $________

APPROVED: Distribution ____________ Payment ____________

Voucher (back)

Exercise 13A3 or 13B3: See pages 256–257.

Exercise 13A4 or 13B4

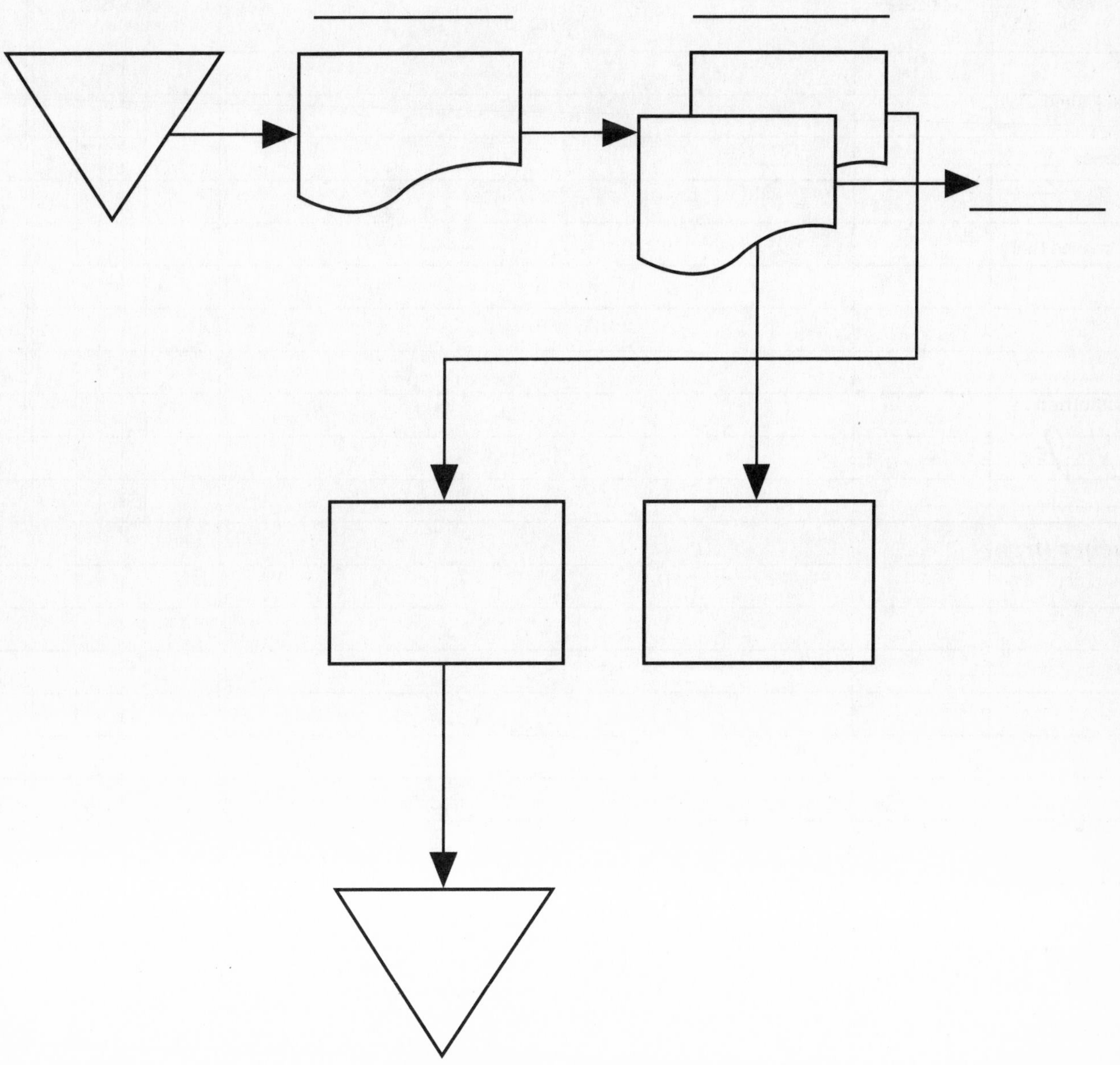

Exercise 13A3 or 13B3

VOUCHER REGISTER FOR MONTH OF 19--

DATE	VOUCHER NO.	ISSUED TO	PURCHASES DR.

Name ______________________________

Exercise 13A3 or 13B3 (Concluded)

PAGE

SUPPLIES DR.	WAGES EXP. DR.	SUNDRY ACCOUNTS DR.			VOUCHERS PAYABLE CR.	PAYMENT	
		ACCOUNT	POST REF.	AMOUNT		DATE	CK. NO.

Exercise 13A5 or 13B5

CHECK REGISTER FOR MONTH OF 19-- PAGE

	DATE	CK. NO.	PAYEE	VOUCHERS PAY. DR. NO.	VOUCHERS PAY. DR. AMOUNT	PURCHASES DISCOUNT CR.	CASH CR.	
1								1
2								2
3								3
4								4
5								5
6								6
7								7
8								8
9								9
10								10
11								11
12								12
13								13

Exercise 13A6 or 13B6

VOUCHER REGISTER FOR MONTH OF 19--

	DATE	VOUCHER NO.	ISSUED TO	PURCHASES DR.	
1					1
2					2
3					3
4					4
5					5
6					6
7					7
8					8
9					9
10					10
11					11
12					12
13					13
14					14

Name ______________________________

Exercise 13A6 or 13B6 (Concluded)

JOURNAL

PAGE

	DATE		DESCRIPTION	POST. REF.	DEBIT	CREDIT	
1							1
2							2
3							3
4							4
5							5
6							6
7							7
8							8
9							9
10							10
11							11
12							12
13							13

PAGE

	SUPPLIES DR.	WAGES EXP. DR.	SUNDRY ACCOUNTS DR.			VOUCHERS PAYABLE CR.	PAYMENT		
			ACCOUNT	POST REF.	AMOUNT		DATE	CK. NO.	
1									1
2									2
3									3
4									4
5									5
6									6
7									7
8									8
9									9
10									10
11									11
12									12
13									13
14									14

Exercise 13A7 or 13B7

Problem 13A1 or 13B1

1.: See pages 262–263.

2.

GENERAL LEDGER

ACCOUNT *Supplies* ACCOUNT NO. *138*

DATE		ITEM	POST. REF.	DEBIT	CREDIT	BALANCE DEBIT	BALANCE CREDIT
19-- July	1	Balance	✓			108 00	

ACCOUNT *Vouchers Payable* ACCOUNT NO. *212*

DATE		ITEM	POST. REF.	DEBIT	CREDIT	BALANCE DEBIT	BALANCE CREDIT

ACCOUNT *Purchases* ACCOUNT NO. *511*

DATE		ITEM	POST. REF.	DEBIT	CREDIT	BALANCE DEBIT	BALANCE CREDIT

ACCOUNT *Rent Expense* ACCOUNT NO. *541*

DATE		ITEM	POST. REF.	DEBIT	CREDIT	BALANCE DEBIT	BALANCE CREDIT

ACCOUNT *Wages Expense* ACCOUNT NO. *544*

DATE		ITEM	POST. REF.	DEBIT	CREDIT	BALANCE DEBIT	BALANCE CREDIT

Problem 13A1 or 13B1 (Continued)

1.

VOUCHER REGISTER FOR MONTH OF 19--

	DATE	VOUCHER NO.	ISSUED TO	PURCHASES DR.	
1					1
2					2
3					3
4					4
5					5
6					6
7					7
8					8
9					9
10					10
11					11
12					12
13					13
14					14
15					15
16					16
17					17
18					18
19					19
20					20
21					21
22					22
23					23
24					24
25					25
26					26
27					27
28					28
29					29
30					30
31					31
32					32

Name ______________________________

Problem 13A1 or 13B1 (Continued)

PAGE 7

	SUPPLIES DR.	WAGES EXP. DR.	SUNDRY ACCOUNTS DR.			VOUCHERS PAYABLE CR.	PAYMENT		
			ACCOUNT	POST REF.	AMOUNT		DATE	CK. NO.	
1									1
2									2
3									3
4									4
5									5
6									6
7									7
8									8
9									9
10									10
11									11
12									12
13									13
14									14
15									15
16									16
17									17
18									18
19									19
20									20
21									21
22									22
23									23
24									24
25									25
26									26
27									27
28									28
29									29
30									30
31									31
32									32

Problem 13A1 or 13B1 (Concluded)

3.

Name ______________________

Problem 13A2 or 13B2

1.

CHECK REGISTER FOR MONTH OF 19-- PAGE *8*

	DATE	CK. NO.	PAYEE	VOUCHERS PAY. DR. NO.	VOUCHERS PAY. DR. AMOUNT	PURCHASES DISCOUNT CR.	CASH CR.	
1								1
2								2
3								3
4								4
5								5
6								6
7								7
8								8
9								9
10								10
11								11

2.

GENERAL LEDGER

ACCOUNT *Cash* ACCOUNT NO. *111*

DATE		ITEM	POST. REF.	DEBIT	CREDIT	BALANCE DEBIT	BALANCE CREDIT
19-- *Aug.*	*1*	*Balance*	✓			*9862 00*	

ACCOUNT *Vouchers Payable* ACCOUNT NO. *212*

DATE		ITEM	POST. REF.	DEBIT	CREDIT	BALANCE DEBIT	BALANCE CREDIT
19-- *Aug.*	*1*	*Balance*	✓				*8482 00*

ACCOUNT *Purchases Discounts* ACCOUNT NO. *511.1*

DATE		ITEM	POST. REF.	DEBIT	CREDIT	BALANCE DEBIT	BALANCE CREDIT

Problem 13A4 or 13B4 (Continued)

1.

VOUCHER REGISTER FOR MONTH OF 19--

	DATE	VOUCHER NO.	ISSUED TO	PURCHASES DR.	
1					1
2					2
3					3
4					4
5					5
6					6
7					7
8					8
9					9
10					10
11					11
12					12
13					13
14					14
15					15
16					16
17					17
18					18
19					19
20					20
21					21
22					22
23					23
24					24
25					25
26					26
27					27
28					28
29					29
30					30
31					31
32					32

Name ____________________

Problem 13A3 or 13B3 (Continued)

PAGE 4

	SUPPLIES DR.	WAGES EXP. DR.	SUNDRY ACCOUNTS DR.			VOUCHERS PAYABLE CR.	PAYMENT		
			ACCOUNT	POST REF.	AMOUNT		DATE	CK. NO.	
1									1
2									2
3									3
4									4
5									5
6									6
7									7
8									8
9									9
10									10
11									11
12									12
13									13
14									14
15									15
16									16
17									17
18									18
19									19
20									20
21									21
22									22
23									23
24									24
25									25
26									26
27									27
28									28
29									29
30									30
31									31
32									32

Problem 13A3 or 13B3 (Continued)

2.

CHECK REGISTER FOR MONTH OF 19-- PAGE 4

	DATE	CK. NO.	PAYEE	VOUCHERS PAY. DR. NO.	VOUCHERS PAY. DR. AMOUNT	PURCHASES DISCOUNT CR.	CASH CR.	
1								1
2								2
3								3
4								4
5								5
6								6
7								7
8								8
9								9
10								10

3.

GENERAL LEDGER

ACCOUNT *Cash* ACCOUNT NO. *111*

DATE		ITEM	POST. REF.	DEBIT	CREDIT	BALANCE DEBIT	BALANCE CREDIT
19-- Apr.	*1*	*Balance*	✓			*5 1 8 9 00*	

ACCOUNT *Supplies* ACCOUNT NO. *138*

DATE		ITEM	POST. REF.	DEBIT	CREDIT	BALANCE DEBIT	BALANCE CREDIT
19-- Apr.	*1*	*Balance*	✓			*4 0 8 00*	

ACCOUNT *Vouchers Payable* ACCOUNT NO. *212*

DATE		ITEM	POST. REF.	DEBIT	CREDIT	BALANCE DEBIT	BALANCE CREDIT

Name ______________________________

Problem 13A3 or 13B3 (Continued)

ACCOUNT *Purchases* ACCOUNT NO. *511*

DATE	ITEM	POST. REF.	DEBIT	CREDIT	BALANCE DEBIT	BALANCE CREDIT

ACCOUNT *Purchases Discounts* ACCOUNT NO. *511.1*

DATE	ITEM	POST. REF.	DEBIT	CREDIT	BALANCE DEBIT	BALANCE CREDIT

ACCOUNT *Rent Expense* ACCOUNT NO. *541*

DATE	ITEM	POST. REF.	DEBIT	CREDIT	BALANCE DEBIT	BALANCE CREDIT

ACCOUNT *Wages Expense* ACCOUNT NO. *544*

DATE	ITEM	POST. REF.	DEBIT	CREDIT	BALANCE DEBIT	BALANCE CREDIT

Problem 13A3 or 13B3 (Concluded)

4.

Name ______________________________

Problem 13A4 or 13B4

1.: See pages 272–273.

2.

CHECK REGISTER FOR MONTH OF 19-- PAGE 5

	DATE	CK. NO.	PAYEE	VOUCHERS PAY. DR.		PURCHASES DISCOUNT CR.	CASH CR.	
				NO.	AMOUNT			
1								1
2								2
3								3
4								4
5								5
6								6
7								7
8								8
9								9
10								10
11								11
12								12
13								13

3.

JOURNAL PAGE 5

	DATE	DESCRIPTION	POST. REF.	DEBIT	CREDIT	
1						1
2						2
3						3
4						4
5						5
6						6
7						7
8						8
9						9
10						10
11						11
12						12
13						13

Problem 13A4 or 13B4 (Continued)

1.

VOUCHER REGISTER FOR MONTH OF 19--

DATE	VOUCHER NO.	ISSUED TO	PURCHASES DR.

Problem 13A4 or 13B4 (Concluded)

PAGE 5

SUPPLIES DR.	WAGES EXP. DR.	SUNDRY ACCOUNTS DR.			VOUCHERS PAYABLE CR.	PAYMENT	
		ACCOUNT	POST REF.	AMOUNT		DATE	CK. NO.

Mastery Problem

1.

VOUCHER REGISTER FOR MONTH OF 19--

DATE	VOUCHER NO.	ISSUED TO	PURCHASES DR.

Name ______________________________

Mastery Problem (Continued)

PAGE *1*

SUPPLIES DR.	WAGES EXP. DR.	SUNDRY ACCOUNTS DR.			VOUCHERS PAYABLE CR.	PAYMENT	
		ACCOUNT	POST. REF.	AMOUNT		DATE	CK. NO.

Mastery Problem (Continued)

CHECK REGISTER FOR MONTH OF 19-- PAGE 1

DATE	CK. NO.	PAYEE	VOUCHERS PAY. DR.		PURCHASES DISCOUNT CR.	CASH CR.
			NO.	AMOUNT		

JOURNAL PAGE 1

DATE		DESCRIPTION	POST. REF.	DEBIT	CREDIT

Mastery Problem (Continued)

2.

GENERAL LEDGER

ACCOUNT *Cash* ACCOUNT NO. *111*

DATE		ITEM	POST. REF.	DEBIT	CREDIT	BALANCE DEBIT	BALANCE CREDIT
19-- July	1	Balance	✓			6 000 00	

ACCOUNT *Supplies* ACCOUNT NO. *151*

DATE		ITEM	POST. REF.	DEBIT	CREDIT	BALANCE DEBIT	BALANCE CREDIT
19-- July	1	Balance	✓			—	—

ACCOUNT *Vouchers Payable* ACCOUNT NO. *218*

DATE		ITEM	POST. REF.	DEBIT	CREDIT	BALANCE DEBIT	BALANCE CREDIT
19-- July	1	Balance	✓			—	—

ACCOUNT *Purchases* ACCOUNT NO. *511*

DATE		ITEM	POST. REF.	DEBIT	CREDIT	BALANCE DEBIT	BALANCE CREDIT
19-- July	1	Balance	✓			—	—

Mastery Problem (Continued)

ACCOUNT *Purchases Discounts* ACCOUNT NO. *511.2*

DATE		ITEM	POST. REF.	DEBIT	CREDIT	BALANCE DEBIT	BALANCE CREDIT
19-- July	1	Balance	✓			—	—

ACCOUNT *Freight-In* ACCOUNT NO. *512*

DATE		ITEM	POST. REF.	DEBIT	CREDIT	BALANCE DEBIT	BALANCE CREDIT
19-- July	1	Balance	✓			—	—

ACCOUNT *Rent Expense* ACCOUNT NO. *541*

DATE		ITEM	POST. REF.	DEBIT	CREDIT	BALANCE DEBIT	BALANCE CREDIT
19-- July	1	Balance	✓			—	—

ACCOUNT *Wages Expense* ACCOUNT NO. *542*

DATE		ITEM	POST. REF.	DEBIT	CREDIT	BALANCE DEBIT	BALANCE CREDIT
19-- July	1	Balance	✓			—	—

Mastery Problem (Concluded)

3.

Name ______________________________

Exercise 14A1 or 14B1

Merchandise Inventory

Income Summary

Exercise 14A2 or 14B2

Exercise 14A3 or 14B3

Cash

Unearned Ticket Revenue

Ticket Revenue

Exercise 14A4 or 14B4

1., 2., and 3.

	ACCOUNT TITLE	ACCT. NO.	TRIAL BALANCE		ADJUSTMENTS		
			DEBIT	CREDIT	DEBIT	CREDIT	
1	*Merchandise Inventory*						1
2	*Income Summary*						2
3	*Purchases*						3
4	*Purchases Returns & Allow.*						4
5	*Purchases Discounts*						5
6							6
7							7
8							8
9							9
10							10
11							11
12							12
13							13
14							14

4.

Exercise 14A4 or 14B4 (Concluded)

	ADJUSTED TRIAL BALANCE		INCOME STATEMENT		BALANCE SHEET		
	DEBIT	CREDIT	DEBIT	CREDIT	DEBIT	CREDIT	
1							1
2							2
3							3
4							4
5							5
6							6
7							7
8							8
9							9
10							10
11							11
12							12
13							13
14							14

Exercise 14A5 or 14B5

Exercise 14A6 or 14B6

JOURNAL PAGE

DATE		DESCRIPTION	POST. REF.	DEBIT	CREDIT

Name ______________________________

Problem 14A1 or 14B1

1. and 2.: See pages 286–287.

3.

JOURNAL PAGE

	DATE		DESCRIPTION	POST. REF.	DEBIT	CREDIT	
1							1
2							2
3							3
4							4
5							5
6							6
7							7
8							8
9							9
10							10
11							11
12							12
13							13
14							14
15							15
16							16
17							17
18							18
19							19
20							20
21							21
22							22
23							23
24							24
25							25
26							26
27							27
28							28
29							29
30							30

Problem 14A1 or 14B1 (Continued)

1. and 2.

	ACCOUNT TITLE	ACCT. NO.	TRIAL BALANCE DEBIT	TRIAL BALANCE CREDIT	ADJUSTMENTS DEBIT	ADJUSTMENTS CREDIT	
1	*Cash*						1
2	*Accounts Receivable*						2
3	*Merchandise Inventory*						3
4	*Supplies*						4
5	*Prepaid Insurance*						5
6	*Land*						6
7	*Building*						7
8	*Accum. Dep.—Building*						8
9	*Store Equipment*						9
10	*Accum. Dep.—Store Eq.*						10
11	*Accounts Payable*						11
12	*Sales Tax Payable*						12
13	*Mortgage Payable*						13
14	*Unearned Revenues*						14
15	*, Capital*						15
16	*, Drawing*						16
17	*Sales*						17
18	*Sales Returns & Allow.*						18
19	*Purchases*						19
20	*Purchases Ret. & Allow.*						20
21	*Purchases Discounts*						21
22	*Freight-In*						22
23	*Wages Expense*						23
24	*Telephone Expense*						24
25	*Utilities Expense*						25
26	*Advertising Expense*						26
27	*Miscellaneous Expense*						27
28							28
29	*Income Summary*						29
30	*Supplies Expense*						30
31	*Insurance Expense*						31
32	*Dep. Expense—Building*						32
33	*Dep. Expense—Store Eq.*						33
34	*Earned Revenue*						34
35	*Wages Payable*						35
36							36
37							37
38							38
39							39
40							40

Problem 14A1 or 14B1 (Concluded)

ADJUSTED TRIAL BALANCE		INCOME STATEMENT		BALANCE SHEET	
DEBIT	CREDIT	DEBIT	CREDIT	DEBIT	CREDIT

Problem 14A2 or 14B2

1. and 2.

	ACCOUNT TITLE	ACCT. NO.	TRIAL BALANCE		ADJUSTMENTS		
			DEBIT	CREDIT	DEBIT	CREDIT	
1	*Cash*						1
2	*Accounts Receivable*						2
3	*Merchandise Inventory*						3
4	*Supplies*						4
5	*Prepaid Insurance*						5
6	*Land*						6
7	*Building*						7
8	*Accum. Dep.—Building*						8
9	*Store Equipment*						9
10	*Accum. Dep.—Store Eq.*						10
11	*Accounts Payable*						11
12	*Sales Tax Payable*						12
13	*Mortgage Payable*						13
14	*Unearned Revenues*						14
15	*, Capital*						15
16	*, Drawing*						16
17	*Sales*						17
18	*Sales Returns & Allow.*						18
19	*Purchases*						19
20	*Purchases Returns & Allow.*						20
21	*Purchases Discounts*						21
22	*Freight-In*						22
23	*Wages Expense*						23
24	*Telephone Expense*						24
25	*Utilities Expense*						25
26	*Advertising Expense*						26
27	*Miscellaneous Expense*						27
28							28
29	*Income Summary*						29
30	*Supplies Expense*						30
31	*Insurance Expense*						31
32	*Dep. Expense—Building*						32
33	*Dep. Expense—Store Eq.*						33
34	*Earned Revenue*						34
35	*Wages Payable*						35
36							36
37							37
38							38
39							39
40							40

Name ________________________________

Problem 14A2 or 14B2 (Continued)

	ADJUSTED TRIAL BALANCE		INCOME STATEMENT		BALANCE SHEET		
	DEBIT	CREDIT	DEBIT	CREDIT	DEBIT	CREDIT	
1							1
2							2
3							3
4							4
5							5
6							6
7							7
8							8
9							9
10							10
11							11
12							12
13							13
14							14
15							15
16							16
17							17
18							18
19							19
20							20
21							21
22							22
23							23
24							24
25							25
26							26
27							27
28							28
29							29
30							30
31							31
32							32
33							33
34							34
35							35
36							36
37							37
38							38
39							39
40							40

Problem 14A2 or 14B2 (Concluded)

3.

JOURNAL PAGE

DATE		DESCRIPTION	POST. REF.	DEBIT	CREDIT

Name ________________________________

Problem 14A3 or 14B3

1.: See pages 292–293.

2.

JOURNAL PAGE

DATE		DESCRIPTION	POST. REF.	DEBIT	CREDIT

Problem 14A3 or 14B3 (Continued)

1.

	ACCOUNT TITLE	ACCT. NO.	TRIAL BALANCE		ADJUSTMENTS		ADJ. TRIAL BALANCE		
			DEBIT	CREDIT	DEBIT	CREDIT	DEBIT	CREDIT	
1	*Cash*								1
2	*Accounts Receivable*								2
3	*Merchandise Inventory*								3
4	*Supplies*								4
5	*Prepaid Insurance*								5
6	*Land*								6
7	*Building*								7
8	*Accum. Dep.—Building*								8
9	*Store Equipment*								9
10	*Accum. Dep.—Store Eq.*								10
11	*Accounts Payable*								11
12	*Sales Tax Payable*								12
13	*Mortgage Payable*								13
14	*Unearned Revenues*								14
15	*, Capital*								15
16	*, Drawing*								16
17	*Sales*								17
18	*Sales Returns & Allow.*								18
19	*Purchases*								19
20	*Purchases Returns & Allow.*								20
21	*Purchases Discounts*								21
22	*Freight-In*								22

Problem 14A3 or 14B3 (Concluded)

23	*Wages Expense*		23
24	*Telephone Expense*		24
25	*Utilities Expense*		25
26	*Advertising Expense*		26
27	*Miscellaneous Expense*		27
28			28
29	*Income Summary*		29
30	*Supplies Expense*		30
31	*Insurance Expense*		31
32	*Dep. Expense—Building*		32
33	*Dep. Expense—Store Eq.*		33
34	*Earned Revenue*		34
35	*Wages Payable*		35
36			36
37			37
38			38
39			39
40			40
41			41
42			42
43			43
44			44

Problem 14A4 or 14B4

ACCOUNT TITLE	ACCT. NO.	TRIAL BALANCE		ADJUSTMENTS	
		DEBIT	CREDIT	DEBIT	CREDIT
Cash					
Accounts Receivable					
Merchandise Inventory					
Supplies					
Prepaid Insurance					
Land					
Building					
Accum. Dep.—Building					
Store Equipment					
Accum. Dep.—Store Equip.					
Accounts Payable					
Sales Tax Payable					
Mortgage Payable					
Unearned Revenues					
, Capital					
, Drawing					
Sales					
Sales Returns & Allowances					
Purchases					
Purchases Returns & Allowances					
Purchases Discounts					
Freight-In					
Wages Expense					
Telephone Expense					
Utilities Expense					
Advertising Expense					
Miscellaneous Expense					
Income Summary					
Supplies Expense					
Insurance Expense					
Depreciation Expense—Building					
Depreciation Expense—Store Equip.					
Earned Revenue					
Wages Payable					

Name ____________________

Problem 14A4 or 14B4 (Continued)

	ADJUSTED TRIAL BALANCE		INCOME STATEMENT		BALANCE SHEET		
	DEBIT	CREDIT	DEBIT	CREDIT	DEBIT	CREDIT	
1							1
2							2
3							3
4							4
5							5
6							6
7							7
8							8
9							9
10							10
11							11
12							12
13							13
14							14
15							15
16							16
17							17
18							18
19							19
20							20
21							21
22							22
23							23
24							24
25							25
26							26
27							27
28							28
29							29
30							30
31							31
32							32
33							33
34							34
35							35
36							36
37							37
38							38
39							39
40							40

Problem 14A4 or 14B4 (Concluded)

JOURNAL

PAGE

DATE		DESCRIPTION	POST. REF.	DEBIT	CREDIT

Name ______________________________

Mastery Problem

1.: See pages 298–299.

2.

JOURNAL PAGE

	DATE		DESCRIPTION	POST. REF.	DEBIT	CREDIT	
1							1
2							2
3							3
4							4
5							5
6							6
7							7
8							8
9							9
10							10
11							11
12							12
13							13
14							14
15							15
16							16
17							17
18							18
19							19
20							20
21							21
22							22
23							23
24							24
25							25
26							26
27							27
28							28
29							29
30							30

Mastery Problem (Continued)

1.

Waikiki

Work

For Year Ended

ACCOUNT TITLE	ACCT. NO.	TRIAL BALANCE DEBIT	TRIAL BALANCE CREDIT	ADJUSTMENTS DEBIT	ADJUSTMENTS CREDIT
Cash		30,000.00			
Accounts Receivable		22,500.00			
Merchandise Inventory		57,000.00			
Supplies		2,700.00			
Prepaid Insurance		3,600.00			
Land		15,000.00			
Building		135,000.00			
Accum. Dep.—Building			24,000.00		
Store Equipment		75,000.00			
Accum. Dep.—Store Eq.			22,500.00		
Notes Payable			7,500.00		
Accounts Payable			15,000.00		
Unearned Rental Revenue			33,000.00		
John Neff, Capital			233,700.00		
John Neff, Drawing		30,000.00			
Sales			300,750.00		
Sales Returns & Allow.		1,800.00			
Purchases		157,500.00			
Purchases Returns & Allow.			1,200.00		
Purchases Discounts			1,500.00		
Freight-In		450.00			
Wages Expense		63,000.00			
Telephone Expense		5,250.00			
Utilities Expense		18,000.00			
Advertising Expense		11,250.00			
Miscellaneous Expense		10,875.00			
Interest Expense		225.00			
		639,150.00	639,150.00		
Income Summary					
Supplies Expense					
Insurance Expense					
Dep. Expense—Building					
Dep. Expense—Store Eq.					
Rental Revenue					
Wages Payable					

Name ______________________________

Mastery Problem (Concluded)

Surf Shop

Sheet

December 31, 19--

ADJUSTED TRIAL BALANCE		INCOME STATEMENT		BALANCE SHEET	
DEBIT	CREDIT	DEBIT	CREDIT	DEBIT	CREDIT

Name ______________________________

Exercise 15A1 or 15B1

Exercise 15A2 or 15B2

Exercise 15A3 or 15B3

Name ______________________________

Exercise 15A4 or 15B4

JOURNAL

PAGE

DATE		DESCRIPTION	POST. REF.	DEBIT	CREDIT

Exercise 15A5 or 15B5

JOURNAL PAGE

	DATE		DESCRIPTION	POST. REF.	DEBIT	CREDIT	
1							1
2							2
3							3
4							4
5							5

Exercise 15A6 or 15B6

DATE	WITHOUT REVERSING ENTRY	WITH REVERSING ENTRY
Adjusting Entry:		
Closing Entry:		
Reversing Entry:		
Payment of Payroll:		

Wages Expense

Wages Expense

Wages Payable

Wages Payable

Name ______________________

Exercise 15A7 or 15B7

Problem 15A1 or 15B1

1.

ACCOUNT TITLE	ACCT. NO.	TRIAL BALANCE		ADJUSTMENTS	
		DEBIT	CREDIT	DEBIT	CREDIT
Cash					
Accounts Receivable					
Merchandise Inventory					
Supplies					
Prepaid Insurance					
Equipment					
Accum. Dep.—Equip.					
Accounts Payable					
Wages Payable					
Sales Tax Payable					
Unearned Revenues					
, Capital					
, Drawing					
Sales					
Sales Returns & Allow.					
Interest Revenue					
Purchases					
Purchases Ret. & Allow.					
Purchases Discounts					
Freight-In					
Wages Expense					
Telephone Expense					
Utilities Expense					
Advertising Expense					
Miscellaneous Expense					
Interest Expense					

Name ______________________________

Problem 15A1 or 15B1 (Continued)

	ADJUSTED TRIAL BALANCE		INCOME STATEMENT		BALANCE SHEET		
	DEBIT	CREDIT	DEBIT	CREDIT	DEBIT	CREDIT	
1							1
2							2
3							3
4							4
5							5
6							6
7							7
8							8
9							9
10							10
11							11
12							12
13							13
14							14
15							15
16							16
17							17
18							18
19							19
20							20
21							21
22							22
23							23
24							24
25							25
26							26
27							27
28							28
29							29
30							30
31							31
32							32
33							33
34							34
35							35
36							36
37							37
38							38
39							39
40							40

Problem 15A1 or 15B1 (Continued)

2., 3., and 4.

JOURNAL

PAGE

DATE		DESCRIPTION	POST. REF.	DEBIT	CREDIT

Name ____________________

Problem 15A1 or 15B1 (Continued)

JOURNAL PAGE

DATE		DESCRIPTION	POST. REF.	DEBIT	CREDIT

Problem 15A1 or 15B1 (Concluded)

5.

Name ______________________________

Problem 15A2 or 15B2

1.

Problem 15A2 or 15B2 (Continued)

2.

Name ______________________________

Problem 15A2 or 15B2 (Concluded)

3.

Problem 15A3 or 15B3

Name ______________________________

Mastery Problem

1.

Mastery Problem (Continued)

2.

Name ______________________________

Mastery Problem (Continued)

3.

Mastery Problem (Continued)

4.

Mastery Problem (Continued)

5.

JOURNAL PAGE

DATE		DESCRIPTION	POST. REF.	DEBIT	CREDIT

Mastery Problem (Concluded)

6. and 7.

JOURNAL

PAGE

DATE	DESCRIPTION	POST. REF.	DEBIT	CREDIT

Name ______________________________

Comprehensive Problem

1. and 3.

GENERAL LEDGER

ACCOUNT *Cash* ACCOUNT NO. *111*

DATE		ITEM	POST. REF.	DEBIT	CREDIT	BALANCE DEBIT	BALANCE CREDIT
19-- Dec.	1	Balance	✓			11,500.00	

ACCOUNT *Accounts Receivable* ACCOUNT NO. *131*

DATE		ITEM	POST. REF.	DEBIT	CREDIT	BALANCE DEBIT	BALANCE CREDIT
19-- Dec.	1	Balance	✓			8,600.00	

ACCOUNT *Merchandise Inventory* ACCOUNT NO. *141*

DATE		ITEM	POST. REF.	DEBIT	CREDIT	BALANCE DEBIT	BALANCE CREDIT
19-- Dec.	1	Balance	✓			21,800.00	

ACCOUNT *Supplies* ACCOUNT NO. *151*

DATE		ITEM	POST. REF.	DEBIT	CREDIT	BALANCE DEBIT	BALANCE CREDIT
19-- Dec.	1	Balance	✓			1,035.00	

ACCOUNT *Prepaid Insurance* ACCOUNT NO. *155*

DATE		ITEM	POST. REF.	DEBIT	CREDIT	BALANCE DEBIT	BALANCE CREDIT
19-- Dec.	1	Balance	✓			1,380.00	

Comprehensive Problem (Continued)

ACCOUNT *Land* ACCOUNT NO. *161*

DATE		ITEM	POST. REF.	DEBIT	CREDIT	BALANCE DEBIT	BALANCE CREDIT
19-- Dec.	1	Balance	✓			8,700 00	

ACCOUNT *Building* ACCOUNT NO. *171*

DATE		ITEM	POST. REF.	DEBIT	CREDIT	BALANCE DEBIT	BALANCE CREDIT
19-- Dec.	1	Balance	✓			52,000 00	

ACCOUNT *Accum. Dep.—Building* ACCOUNT NO. *171.1*

DATE		ITEM	POST. REF.	DEBIT	CREDIT	BALANCE DEBIT	BALANCE CREDIT
19-- Dec.	1	Balance	✓				9,200 00

ACCOUNT *Store Equipment* ACCOUNT NO. *181*

DATE		ITEM	POST. REF.	DEBIT	CREDIT	BALANCE DEBIT	BALANCE CREDIT
19-- Dec.	1	Balance	✓			28,750 00	

ACCOUNT *Accum. Dep.—Store Equip.* ACCOUNT NO. *181.1*

DATE		ITEM	POST. REF.	DEBIT	CREDIT	BALANCE DEBIT	BALANCE CREDIT
19-- Dec.	1	Balance	✓				9,300 00

Name ______________________________

Comprehensive Problem (Continued)

ACCOUNT *Accounts Payable* ACCOUNT NO. *218*

DATE		ITEM	POST. REF.	DEBIT	CREDIT	BALANCE DEBIT	BALANCE CREDIT
19-- Dec.	1	Balance	✓				6,850.00

ACCOUNT *Sales Tax Payable* ACCOUNT NO. *221*

DATE		ITEM	POST. REF.	DEBIT	CREDIT	BALANCE DEBIT	BALANCE CREDIT
19-- Dec.	1	Balance	✓				970.00

ACCOUNT *Mortgage Payable* ACCOUNT NO. *231*

DATE		ITEM	POST. REF.	DEBIT	CREDIT	BALANCE DEBIT	BALANCE CREDIT
19-- Dec.	1	Balance	✓				12,525.00

ACCOUNT *Tom Jones, Capital* ACCOUNT NO. *311*

DATE		ITEM	POST. REF.	DEBIT	CREDIT	BALANCE DEBIT	BALANCE CREDIT
19-- Dec.	1	Balance	✓				90,000.00

ACCOUNT *Tom Jones, Drawing* ACCOUNT NO. *312*

DATE		ITEM	POST. REF.	DEBIT	CREDIT	BALANCE DEBIT	BALANCE CREDIT
19-- Dec.	1	Balance	✓			8,500.00	

Comprehensive Problem (Continued)

ACCOUNT *Sales* ACCOUNT NO. *411*

DATE		ITEM	POST. REF.	DEBIT	CREDIT	BALANCE DEBIT	BALANCE CREDIT
19-- Dec.	1	Balance	✓				116 0 0 0 00

ACCOUNT *Sales Returns and Allowances* ACCOUNT NO. *411.1*

DATE		ITEM	POST. REF.	DEBIT	CREDIT	BALANCE DEBIT	BALANCE CREDIT
19-- Dec.	1	Balance	✓			6 9 0 00	

ACCOUNT *Purchases* ACCOUNT NO. *511*

DATE		ITEM	POST. REF.	DEBIT	CREDIT	BALANCE DEBIT	BALANCE CREDIT
19-- Dec.	1	Balance	✓			60 5 0 0 00	

ACCOUNT *Purchases Returns and Allowances* ACCOUNT NO. *511.1*

DATE		ITEM	POST. REF.	DEBIT	CREDIT	BALANCE DEBIT	BALANCE CREDIT
19-- Dec.	1	Balance	✓				4 6 0 00

ACCOUNT *Purchases Discounts* ACCOUNT NO. *511.2*

DATE		ITEM	POST. REF.	DEBIT	CREDIT	BALANCE DEBIT	BALANCE CREDIT
19-- Dec.	1	Balance	✓				5 7 5 00

Name ____________________

Comprehensive Problem (Continued)

ACCOUNT *Freight-In* ACCOUNT NO. *512*

DATE		ITEM	POST. REF.	DEBIT	CREDIT	BALANCE DEBIT	BALANCE CREDIT
19-- Dec.	1	Balance	✓			1 7 5 00	

ACCOUNT *Wages Expense* ACCOUNT NO. *542*

DATE		ITEM	POST. REF.	DEBIT	CREDIT	BALANCE DEBIT	BALANCE CREDIT
19-- Dec.	1	Balance	✓			25 0 0 0 00	

ACCOUNT *Telephone Expense* ACCOUNT NO. *545*

DATE		ITEM	POST. REF.	DEBIT	CREDIT	BALANCE DEBIT	BALANCE CREDIT
19-- Dec.	1	Balance	✓			2 0 0 0 00	

ACCOUNT *Utilities Expense* ACCOUNT NO. *549*

DATE		ITEM	POST. REF.	DEBIT	CREDIT	BALANCE DEBIT	BALANCE CREDIT
19-- Dec.	1	Balance	✓			6 9 0 0 00	

ACCOUNT *Advertising Expense* ACCOUNT NO. *551*

DATE		ITEM	POST. REF.	DEBIT	CREDIT	BALANCE DEBIT	BALANCE CREDIT
19-- Dec.	1	Balance	✓			4 3 0 0 00	

Comprehensive Problem (Continued)

ACCOUNT *Miscellaneous Expense* ACCOUNT NO. *572*

DATE		ITEM	POST. REF.	DEBIT	CREDIT	BALANCE DEBIT	BALANCE CREDIT
19-- Dec.	1	Balance	✓			2,700.00	

ACCOUNT *Interest Expense* ACCOUNT NO. *581*

DATE		ITEM	POST. REF.	DEBIT	CREDIT	BALANCE DEBIT	BALANCE CREDIT
19-- Dec.	1	Balance	✓			1,350.00	

ACCOUNTS RECEIVABLE LEDGER

NAME *Martha Boyle* TERMS

ADDRESS *12 Jude Lane, Hartford, CT 06117*

DATE		ITEM	POST. REF.	DEBIT	CREDIT	BALANCE
19-- Dec.	1	Balance	✓			3,250.00

NAME *Anne Clark* TERMS

ADDRESS *52 Juniper Road, Hartford, CT 06118*

DATE		ITEM	POST. REF.	DEBIT	CREDIT	BALANCE
19-- Dec.	1	Balance	✓			1,340.00

Name ______________________________

Comprehensive Problem (Continued)

NAME *John Dempsey* TERMS

ADDRESS *700 Hobbes Dr., Avon, CT 06108*

DATE		ITEM	POST. REF.	DEBIT	CREDIT	BALANCE
19-- Dec.	1	Balance	✓			1 5 6 0 00

NAME *Lucy Greene* TERMS

ADDRESS *236 Bally Lane, Simsbury, CT 06123*

DATE		ITEM	POST. REF.	DEBIT	CREDIT	BALANCE
19-- Dec.	1	Balance	✓			1 9 6 0 00

NAME *Heather Waters* TERMS

ADDRESS *447 Drury Lane, West Hartford, CT 06107*

DATE		ITEM	POST. REF.	DEBIT	CREDIT	BALANCE
19-- Dec.	1	Balance	✓			4 9 0 00

NAME *Kim Fields* TERMS

ADDRESS *5200 Hamilton Ave., Hartford, CT 06117*

DATE		ITEM	POST. REF.	DEBIT	CREDIT	BALANCE

Comprehensive Problem (Continued)

ACCOUNTS PAYABLE LEDGER

NAME *Jerry Evans* TERMS

ADDRESS *34 Harry Ave., East Hartford, CT 06234*

DATE		ITEM	POST. REF.	DEBIT	CREDIT	BALANCE
19-- Dec.	1	Balance	✓			1 2 5 0 00

NAME *Peter Nathen* TERMS

ADDRESS *1009 Drake Rd., Farmington, CT 06082*

DATE		ITEM	POST. REF.	DEBIT	CREDIT	BALANCE
19-- Dec.	1	Balance	✓			3 0 0 0 00

NAME *James Owen* TERMS

ADDRESS *43 Lucky Lane, Bristol, CT 06007*

DATE		ITEM	POST. REF.	DEBIT	CREDIT	BALANCE
19-- Dec.	1	Balance	✓			1 6 0 0 00

NAME *Harold West* TERMS

ADDRESS *888 Anders Street, Newington, CT 06789*

DATE		ITEM	POST. REF.	DEBIT	CREDIT	BALANCE
19-- Dec.	1	Balance	✓			1 0 0 0 00

Name ______________________________

Comprehensive Problem (Continued)

2.

SALES JOURNAL PAGE 6

DATE		SALE NO.	TO WHOM SOLD	POST REF.	ACCOUNTS RECEIVABLE DR.	SALES CR.	SALES TAX PAYABLE CR.

PURCHASES JOURNAL PAGE 5

	DATE		INVOICE NO.	FROM WHOM PURCHASED	POST REF.	PURCHASES DR. ACCTS. PAY. CR.	
1							1
2							2
3							3
4							4
5							5
6							6
7							7
8							8
9							9
10							10
11							11
12							12
13							13
14							14

Comprehensive Problem (Continued)

CASH RECEIPTS JOURNAL

PAGE 9

DATE	ACCOUNT CREDITED	POST REF.	GENERAL CR.	ACCOUNTS RECEIV. CR.	SALES CR.	SALES TAX PAY. CR.	CASH DR.

JOURNAL

PAGE 4

DATE	DESCRIPTION	POST. REF.	DEBIT	CREDIT

Comprehensive Problem (Continued)

CASH PAYMENTS JOURNAL

PAGE *10*

DATE	CK. NO.	ACCOUNT DEBITED	POST REF.	GENERAL DR.	ACCOUNTS PAYABLE DR.	PURCHASES DR.	PURCHASES DISC. CR.	CASH CR.

Comprehensive Problem (Continued)

4.

Name ____________________

Comprehensive Problem (Continued)

5.

Comprehensive Problem (Continued)

TJ's Specialty

Work

For Year Ended

ACCOUNT TITLE	ACCT. NO.	TRIAL BALANCE		ADJUSTMENTS	
		DEBIT	CREDIT	DEBIT	CREDIT
Cash	*111*				
Accounts Receivable	*131*				
Merchandise Inventory	*141*				
Supplies	*151*				
Prepaid Insurance	*155*				
Land	*161*				
Building	*171*				
Accum. Dep.—Building	*171.1*				
Store Equipment	*181*				
Accum. Dep.—Store Equip.	*181.1*				
Accounts Payable	*218*				
Sales Tax Payable	*221*				
Mortgage Payable	*231*				
Tom Jones, Capital	*311*				
Tom Jones, Drawing	*312*				
Sales	*411*				
Sales Returns & Allow.	*411.1*				
Purchases	*511*				
Purchases Ret. & Allow.	*511.1*				
Purchases Discounts	*511.2*				
Freight-In	*512*				
Wages Expense	*542*				
Telephone Expense	*545*				
Utilities Expense	*549*				
Advertising Expense	*551*				
Miscellaneous Expense	*572*				
Interest Expense	*581*				

Name ______________________________

Comprehensive Problem (Continued)

Shop

Sheet

December 31, 19--

	ADJUSTED TRIAL BALANCE		INCOME STATEMENT		BALANCE SHEET		
	DEBIT	CREDIT	DEBIT	CREDIT	DEBIT	CREDIT	
1							1
2							2
3							3
4							4
5							5
6							6
7							7
8							8
9							9
10							10
11							11
12							12
13							13
14							14
15							15
16							16
17							17
18							18
19							19
20							20
21							21
22							22
23							23
24							24
25							25
26							26
27							27
28							28
29							29
30							30
31							31
32							32
33							33
34							34
35							35
36							36
37							37
38							38
39							39
40							40

Comprehensive Problem (Continued)

Comprehensive Problem (Continued)

Comprehensive Problem (Continued)

6.

JOURNAL PAGE *5*

DATE		DESCRIPTION	POST. REF.	DEBIT	CREDIT

Name ________________________________

Comprehensive Problem (Concluded)

7. and 8.

JOURNAL PAGE 6

DATE		DESCRIPTION	POST. REF.	DEBIT	CREDIT